REAL ESTATE

TABLE OF CONTENTS

INTRODUCTION

Many of us aren't going to be rich or millionaires from just working on our jobs. We have a little amount of time for active working. To achieve our financial independence, we have to develop alternative sources of passive income. Real estate investing can generate big profits and multiply your net worth.

Just like investing in the stock market, real estate investing can also be exhausting. However, there are just a few fundamentals that you need to master before you get started.

When you invest in real estate, you expect that the money you put to work today should grow to more money in the future. For many people, real estate is a great option to diversify their portfolio and generate some income at the time of retirement, or even beginning a new career.

Investing in real estate may appear as something only the rich can do. But the fact is that daily investors can always invest in real estate. You may not purchase a multi-million-dollar property, but you can invest in a starter house, clear the mortgage, and then rent it for some profit when you purchase the next house.

Real estate can be a bit complex than just buying mutual funds using 401(k). So, while daily investors can channel their money into real estate, you shouldn't do so until you have a plan that guides you on what you are doing. In this book, you will be guided on the steps you should take to invest in real estate. The first chapter will look at the basics of real estate, to give you a clue of what you should expect in the rest of the chapters.

CHAPTER 1

Introduction to real estate investment

Real estate investment is considered by many as the easiest form of investment. One of the reasons is that there is a good exchange between the tenant and landlord. As long as the place of stay is good, and the landlord receives his or her due on time, life runs smoothly. But real estate investment is a bit complex than this.

If you make up your mind to invest in real estate, your goal is to invest your money and grow it so that you earn more. You have generated enough profit that will cover up any risks and other costs of owning a real estate property. This chapter will introduce to you the basics of real estate to help you gain a rough idea of how investors make income from their real estate enterprises.

In most cases, people start real estate investment to secure their future. Additionally, some set up real estate businesses as a passive income investment. In other words, real estate investment supplements their main source of income. Besides other investments, investors have dived into properties such as apartment units, houses, and other forms of real estate to expand their portfolios, earn more income, and plan for their retirement.

Some people look at the home they currently stay as an investment, which may appreciate after a few years if the housing prices rise. Others may invest in real estate by buying property to lease to a business to earn income via the rental payments that the individual provides. This is referred to as investing in "real property' and is one of the easiest methods to generate income through real estate.

Investing in real estate is far much better than the traditional investment system. In the traditional investment system, the property owner has the responsibility to process all the paperwork, search for a tenant, and perform any repairs. Owners of property are still accountable for all costs tied to the property.

Since the traditional system of real estate investment demands time, and money to pay for the property, it is better to invest in real estate using trusts, and other forms of investments that don't demand your time. When you invest through trusts, you don't need to maintain and manage properties. Instead, there are people employed to do this on your behalf.

So, why should you invest in real estate?

In recent years, people have joined real estate investment as a means for alternative income, and gaining profits that they may never have achieved through normal investments like bonds and stocks.

So, real estate investment is a far better investment that can provide a continuous stream of income over a specific time. Rent is a fixed income that you agree with the tenant, and you get paid every month.

Investment in real estate can still be a means to diversify an investment portfolio. Adding real estate investment into a portfolio of diversified assets, it can regulate the whole risk, and thus help investors to eliminate risks in their portfolios without affecting returns.

These features make real estate investment an efficient tool to diversify portfolios. However, just like all investments, there must be risks and uncertainties, real estate investment is not an exception; you have to be ready for some serious.

The 5 big reasons why real estate investment is awesome.

1. Income

This was going to come first because it's the main reason why everyone wants to take part in real estate investment. If you follow every step correctly, real estate can generate a huge stream of income that is enough to pay all your bills and save for your future.

If you own several multi-family buildings, each of the units occupied by tenants creates a stream of income. The tenants pay rent at the end of each month, and that income flows to the owner account.

This point is important because it defines the long-term.

Many people have a goal to save for retirement. Therefore, they try as much as they can to save enough money so that one day, they can replace the current income with their job, and stop working.

In other words, every time you buy a real estate that pays you a certain income you move a step close to your goal of income replacement.

You only need to get to a point where the income you earn from your properties is enough that you don't need to work anymore.

And then you can call it quits to your 9-5 job.

One of the main problems that people experience when they are planning for retirement is how to build a stream of income so that they stop working.

People work for years to create a retirement "nest-egg," and then they fail to identify the best way to turn the "nest- egg" into a running stream of income. But real estate is the answer to this problem.

2. Depreciation

Depreciation is an accounting technique that will allow you to reduce the value of an asset over its life.

For example, assume a farmer who buys a tractor to support his or her business. The reality is that the tractor is only going to last for several years until the farmer may have to buy another one. In this case, the IRS lets the farmer cut a certain percent of the cost of the tractor from their taxes every year as a business expense.

But the magic of real estate is that you also reduce the value of the property, but with time real estate rises in value as opposed to the tractor which becomes worthless.

As a result, you get a tax reduction to offset the income the property is generating for you, allowing you to save money over time. That is awesome.

3. Equity

Every time you pay for the mortgage, part of it is used to pay interest on the loan and another percent is used to pay down the principal value of the property. For every payment you make, you own more of the property.

If you own different rental properties, and all are occupied with tenants, the income you get from the rentals will pay your mortgage investment, and the remaining amount will be used for repair, maintenance, and other needs.

When you are done with the mortgage, you will own the whole rental property, and your tenants will have paid for most of the cost.

4. Appreciation

Besides the build-up in equity from paying down the mortgage, you will also earn from the rise in property value. After some years, the real estate prices increase in value. For example, between the 1960s and 2000s, there has never been a single year of decline in median home properties in the U.S.

Every part of the country is a bit different, but besides the high-appreciating places like popular cities, inflation also increases the prices of things over time including real estate.

5. Leverage

Leverage is a technique that you can pay for something without cashing out the entire cost. For the case of real estate, you can apply leverage by including mortgage to purchase a property and only pay a fraction of the total cost.

Though you only pay a small percentage of the buying price, you are accountable for All the benefits.

You will still earn all the income generated, all the equity created, all the appreciation of the property, and you make use of all the tax write-offs.

This is something that you can't achieve with other types of investments. There are few methods to purchase financial investments using leverage beyond the margin account, and there are other problems to worry about when you use it. But that is not going to be covered here.

The acquisition of leverage in the real estate market is what allows you to begin investing before you amass a fortune.

Different ways to invest in real estate

Now that you know the reason why you should invest in real estate; here's how you can get started. There are a lot of options available for you if you want to start in real estate investing.

1. Real estate investment trusts (REITS)

REITS own and run the real estate. They own large properties like office buildings, apartments, warehouses, and shopping malls. REITS are different from other real estate companies because they don't build properties to resell later, but their goal is to buy real estate properties to manage.

This means if you decide to invest in REIT, you will be eligible to earn income through payouts that trusts get from the properties they own. Investment in REITs can either be public or private.

For the public REITs, they are often exchanged on public platforms. For private REITs, the shares aren't posted on an exchange platform but are sold in an exclusive market. This is why they are very risky than public REITs. Being an investor, you have to fulfill certain requirements before you can start to invest as a private REIT.

Whether you invest in private or public REITs, both have risks that might impact the investment. Since private REITs aren't available in public, they have a higher risk than public REITs.

Risks of public REITS

Changes in rates of interest

When the rate of interest increases, REITs make less profit, and the reason is that their demand goes down. In this case, you will need to stick to your investment for some time.

Rental risk

REITs depend on rent they collect from real estate property they run. In this case, when a property owned by REIT remains unoccupied for a long period, the profit earned by REITs is affected. This translates to lower income paid to investors.

Risks in private REITs

Low liquidity

Private REITS aren't available in public. Therefore, it's hard to know the exact value, and it can't be easily traded. As an investor, you have to hold on to your investment for some time.

No transparency

Unlike public REITs that are subject to disclosure requirements, private REITs aren't. In fact, there is little information on how private REITs run. As a result, it is not easy to know how the REIT is performing.

Reduction in investment value

The payouts you earn and the value of the investment are affected by the property value invested by the RIET. In other words, if there are tenants who don't pay their rents or higher rates of vacancy may impact the number of payments.

Personal liability

You may be held accountable for clearing the requirements of private REIT if the REIT doesn't have funds to meet its costs. This is referred to as "capital call."

2. Real estate limited partnerships

These are also known as "LPS," and are popular for building and managing property already built.

LPs are under the supervision of a general partner. This individual uses the money collected from investors to buy land, and build properties. They can still sell it at a higher price than what they bought.

For investors, they can buy units in real estate LPS. A lot of these units are private and aren't traded on an exchange. Additionally, they are difficult to estimate the value or even resell it.

Common risks of investing in real estate LPs

No guarantee

Since the value of real estate changes with time, it's not a must that every project you invest in will generate profit.

Operational risks

Real estate LP depends fully on the ability of the management that support the partnership. For that reason, investors have a passive responsibility and are limited to the investment they have made. In other words, investors have no active role in the business partnership.

No diversification

Some real estate LPs develop single projects for a given period. Therefore, if the project is partially done, you might lose a specific percent of your investment.

Approvals of the government

Some real estate LPS don't have government permits to allow them to build on their land. Sometimes, they are denied permits, and this affects the investment value.

Risk of capital

Projects that go past the set budget may force you to invest more money to cover extra costs.

Mortgage investment entities

These are mortgage finances that tap money from investors to loan individuals who may fail to acquire a mortgage from traditional lenders such as credit unions.

Mortgage investment entities (MIEs) offer loans to borrowers using money collected from investors. These loans build the portfolio of a MIE and consist of residential mortgages like family houses, condominiums, townhouses, and commercial mortgages.

MIEs make money from the mortgage interest, mortgage renewals, financing fees, cancellation penalties, and other fees deducted from borrowers.

If you are an investor, you buy security produced by the MIE, essentially in the form of shares, restricted partnership units, or even trust units. These securities acquire value from the value of the underlying pool of mortgages secured by the real estate properties. You are allowed to get income from the revenue received by the MIE via its portfolio of mortgages.

Majority of the MIEs are private and don't have their securities listed on an exchange, making it hard to trade and value.

Risks of investing in MIEs

High-risk loans

MIEs usually offer mortgages that have a higher risk than mortgages generated by banks. In case a lot of borrowers fail to make their mortgage payments, the value your investment can drop, and the MIE may fail to offer you with any income.

Lack of liquidity

Most MIEs are private and not publicly traded, and that may make it hard to value and cannot be resold easily. You might have to stick to your investment for longer than you may have planned.

No guarantee

Certain MIEs claim to provide high annual yields and market investments 'secured by real property.' Secured doesn't imply that it's guaranteed, and though the real estate might directly support the mortgage, your investment isn't secured. Therefore, you don't have any rights to the property that secures the mortgage.

In case a borrower fails to make payments on a mortgage, this can damage the strength of the MIE to manage payments to investors and will affect the value of the investment. There are still many factors that can affect the success of and profits from a MIE. Past performance doesn't indicate the future returns of an investment.

High-risk loans

MIEs usually generate mortgages that have a higher risk than mortgages made by credit unions. If many borrowers don't pay their mortgage, the value of the investment drops and the MIE may fail to generate any income.

Drop in investment value

Borrowers can default on their mortgages or repay it sooner than expected, both of which can impact the value of your investment or even the amount of income that is paid out to you.

Low priority of rights

Borrowers can get second, or third MIE mortgages, which can be a bit risky. So, if a borrower doesn't pay for their mortgage, and the property is liquidated, the lender that released the first mortgage will be the first in the queue to receive the money back. The MIE that offered the second mortgage will only get the money back when the first mortgage is completely paid off.

Syndicated mortgages

These types of mortgages are offered by two or more investors that have invested directly in a single mortgage property.

As opposed to MIE investment, a syndicated mortgage investment only works for a single mortgage, instead of a portfolio mortgage. Some syndicated mortgages are used to support large-scale real estate development projects, for example, a high-rise condo building.

Risks of investing in a syndicated mortgage investment

There is no guarantee of high return

Though some syndicated mortgage investments may claim to provide 'guaranteed' high returns, these claims are false and not authorized by the law. All investments have a specific risk, and the higher the probability rate of return, the higher the risk of investment.

Secured doesn't imply it's guaranteed

Certain syndicated mortgages are said to be 'safe,' or 'fully secured.' Though it's true that your investment will be used to build a mortgage that is registered and secured with a building, if anything goes wrong with the project, and the value of the investment is restricted to the value of the land-you could rank behind other lenders and you may fail to receive any or all your money back. The reason is that the value of the land could only be sufficient to pay any prior ranking lenders.

A queue for repayment

If you are a syndicated mortgage investor, you will always come second in line to receive your payment. In this case, if the project fails to go through, you may not have any money left over to be paid.

Interest payment risks

A syndicated mortgage borrower may not have all the sources of income to facilitate the mortgage's interest payments. If you are an investor, you will be dependent on the borrower to get extra financing.

Lack of investor protection insurance

The government or investor protection fund doesn't ensure the syndicated mortgages. This means that there is no means for you to get your money back.

Early withdrawals

In case you want to withdraw your money before the end of the term, a new investor may be required to take over your position, and there is no guarantee that there shall be an additional for resale.

CHAPTER 2

Finding Investment Properties

There are various types of rental properties in the real estate market. Each has its own advantages and drawbacks, and some do well in certain conditions than others.

To choose the best type of property for your investment, there are a few factors that you need to consider, and most importantly, some investment strategies work well for specific types of properties than others.

When you decide to invest in real estate, you may encounter different investment properties. But how can you choose the best investment property type perfect for your needs?

There are a wide variety of factors that will impact your decision including the size of your budget, property location, and many more.

In this section, you will start by learning the different residential property types and what's special about them and then look at the different investment methods and the types of investment properties that will match every strategy.

Single-Family Homes

These homes have detached dwellings that host a small number of people. Single-family homes are the type of residential located outside the metropolitan city in the US, and they are often surrounded by a yard. In addition, they have their own drive-through and appear attractive to all types of tenants.

In the urban sides, single-family homes can be a bit expensive because they occupy a massive piece of land than other types of residential properties. However, because single-family homes are popular in suburban places, they are somehow cheap considering that they have a yard that surrounds them, and in most cases, they have a private swimming pool.

Townhouses

These are popular in larger cities. They feature a terraced house and contain a small footprint on several floors. Though they are small in size, townhouses have an extensive living space because they consist of multiple floors, which may rise to 6 or more floors in certain places.

Townhouses can be more expensive where single-family homes are rare. This is common in cities where a piece of land is more expensive than in the suburbs.

Condominiums

Also known as condos, they are the most common type of non-apartments in metropolitan and urban cities. Condominiums are divided into different units over a massive piece of land, and they are often surrounded by common places such as swimming pools and private parks shared by individuals of the condo complex.

In general, condos are cheaper than other types of residential properties, but they also have rules and regulations when it comes to maintenance, taxes, and insurance.

Luxury homes

Luxury homes are modern homes designed to be comfy. There are different descriptions of what a luxurious home should look, with some people defining it based on where it is situated, size and architectural design. Despite this, luxury homes share one thing in common: they are more expensive.

In fact, they are the most expensive types of residential properties. In most cases, luxury homes are located in upper-class locations and beautiful places such as Miami Beach.

Apartment

An apartment refers to a self-contained house unit that occupies a given space of a building. Apartment is flexible, lower upfront expenses and free maintenance. Apartments exist of different sizes; some are large while others are smaller.

Bungalow

You have probably heard of a bungalow, right? If not, these are low homes that feature an extended front porch without any upper floor or upper rooms defined in the roof. One unique thing with bungalow is that they make it easy for the elderly, and little children because they have a single floor.

Beds and breakfast

These are private homes designed for guests to spend a night. It consists of an inclusive breakfast along with other special amenities. Bed and breakfast are special and differ by city and region. They offer a much better value than a hotel because of better amenities such as Wi-Fi, parking, room, and bath.

Cabin

In the past, a cabin used to be a small home developed from logs. But today a cabin refers to a vacation home. It is a one-story home. Cabins are known for being warm, cozy and relaxing.

Chalet

Chalets resemble cabins except that they are built with heavier angled roofs and paneled sides. In addition, they have been linked with mountain locales.

Cottage

A cottage as the name suggests is a small home. Cottages are constructed using different types of materials such as wood, wattle, and stone. Cottages are popular in rural and semi-rural areas.

Mansion

Mansion are large and expensive houses.

Hostel

Hostels are pocket-friendly rental properties that are shared by travelers. 4-20 travelers can share a room at a time. Hostels are affordable and offer the chance to interact with different people from all walks of life.

Studio

A studio apartment is a tiny apartment. This apartment comprises of a living room, kitchen, and bedroom that is merged into a single room. Studio apartments are cheap and efficient. Because the studios have a minimum space, this type of accommodation is convenient for a single person.

Different investment strategies

There a few investment strategies that every investor in real estate would prefer. Each investment technique carries its own pros and cons when you evaluate it based on the risk level, profit, and the amount of time required for every technique to happen.

Here are the three popular strategies including the advantages and disadvantages.

Long-term rental

These are the most popular investment strategies common for entry-level investments and new investors. Long-term renting is a method of investment that depends on buying a real estate property for the main goal of renting it out for 6 or more months. The property owner and the landlord would sign a rental lease with the tenants renting the house, and the tenants would start to pay a monthly rent to the landlord which can be used to handle the property expenses, taxes, mortgage, and insurance.

Long-term rentals are best for townhouses and single-family homes. Typically, they feature the lowest risk of any investment strategy, and once the mortgage is cleared, they can begin to generate a large amount of rental income every month.

The disadvantage of long-term rentals is that it requires a lot of commitment and time before it begins to produce a substantial profit.

Short-term rental

This type of properties resembles traditional rentals. However, a short-term rental is offered for a short period, usually days, months, or weeks. This kind of rental properties has become more common in the past years because of the rise of services, websites, and companies such as HomeAway, Airbnb, and VRBO.

The short-term rentals usually take advantage of all types of real estate properties, but the luxurious houses can be more profitable because of the above-average rental rates that a landlord can charge his or her tenants.

The biggest drawback of these type of properties arises from the fact that different cities in the US have specific laws and regulations that limit this investment technique. Therefore, it's illegal to rent out properties for short periods or allow it for a limited period every year.

Fix-and-flip

Fix-and-flip properties are the types of real estate properties that are in a bad state and require substantial renovations and repair before they return to a condition good for stay. This investment technique can be a better option for a real estate investor wanting to earn a quick profit on their investment type. However, they also feature a high percentage of risk because of the high amount of charges that have to be invested in improving the property and the unexpected costs that may emerge in the whole investment.

Condos are a perfect option for a fix-and-flip method because of the tiny size condos and affordable costs of renovation. However, any residential property can be a perfect choice for a fix-and-flip, excluding luxury houses.

While certain types of properties may perform well for specific strategies of an investment than others, they are always great opportunities in the real estate market that can be perfect for your unique type of investment.

What type of property is the best for rental?

Choosing the wrong type of property is like marrying a wrong wife. It can be very stressful, difficult to end the marriage, and damaging to your whole life.

But how can you tell the best property to choose? Probably questions such as:

What should you purchase? What things should you avoid?

Should you go for four or two bedrooms? How about garages?

Is color important?

These are some of the most popular questions that you ask when you are about to purchase the correct deal and have the highest success as a landlord. Well, let's look at some things that you need to consider when you shop for a rental property.

Remember, everything being discussed here relies on the current trends in your location. In addition, this list isn't a bunch of rules that you need to adhere, but only tips that can serve you well.

Let's begin:

Bedrooms

Sometimes, it's hard to find long-term tenants in a 1-2-bedroom house. Single tenants prefer a one-bedroom, but when they hook up with a cute lady, they now need to move into a big bedroom such as two-bedroom. After some years, they get children and now need to move into a three-bedroom house. Therefore, three or four-bedroom house make the best rentals because they attract long-term tenants, reducing your vacancy expenses. Additionally, three- bedroom homes are the perfect type of property to sell, which can be the best when the time arrives.

If you are looking for a multifamily unit, two-bedroom houses are typically acceptable and popular. Single bedroom and studio are also prevalent but usually, attract many transient tenants.

Alternatively, more bedrooms aren't always a better choice. If you extend to five-bedroom homes or even more, you'll realize that the only tenants who want to rent them are families with many kinds. While kids are interesting and playful, many kids on property results in cases of broken windows, stained carpet and many more challenges. Therefore, you should try to keep a house to three-four bedrooms.

Age

If you purchase a very old property, be ready to pay a lot of costs in maintenance and fixing. Older houses also save less energy than new houses, which can increase utility bills. You may assume that it's not important because tenants are going to pay for their cooling and heating, but the truth is that tenants are aware of this. Therefore, if your property will cost an extra $100 to cool or hear, your tenants will do some simple math, and you may have a huge problem to maintain tenants in your property. This doesn't mean that you stop investing in older homes, but you just need to be aware that the older home, the more issues you will need to address.

Garage

When you decide to invest in single-family homes, it can be stressful to get a stable, long-term tenant to accept to live in a house that has no garage. Tenants usually accumulate a lot of things, and they need somewhere to keep them. Plus, places that experience a specific amount of rain, tenants enjoy the luxury of parking in a garage.

Homes that have garages stay occupied for longer than homes without garages.

Utilities

Certain properties, in particular, old houses, have utilities paid by the property owner, which is not a great option.

When you have little control over the house, adds a headache to your life. When tenants don't pay for the energy, they tend to misuse things. If they don't pay for water bills, they may never tell you about the leaking pipe in the bathroom costing you some hundred dollars every year.

For that reason, when you are searching for a single-family home, go for the ones which the tenant can pay utilities. When you look for multi-family homes, pick the ones where the tenant can pay heat and electricity, and if you can get properties that can be transformed into a "master metered" system that will permit tenants to pay for their water, you will have won for yourself some gold.

Lawn

Certain properties with gardens, large lawn, and other external amenities may never be attended with the same care as you would have done. Though every rule has some exceptions, it's good to look for properties with a small yard. That aside, recreational space is key in attracting a long-term tenant. So you should ensure that the tenant has a place where she can go to have some fun with the kids.

Parking

Stable tenants should have a place where they can park their vehicles. A driveway or even a garage is something that tenants like, so you should always look for properties with the above features. In general, two parking locations are far better than one, and so on.

Location

When looking for a property, keep a close eye on what's around. A tenant is just like you: they will want a place to eat out often, they will want to take a walk in the park, and they will want to buy some milk in the grocery store. They will also want to take their children to a great school, and commute less to their job.

They don't want to be hijacked, or stolen from. So you should purchase properties in places where tenants want to stay, and you will earn a stable rental income.

These are some of the features of property types that you should consider when purchasing a rental property. It is not a must to get each right to find a great rental property, but these aspects are crucial to pay attention to when looking for a property.

How to find investment properties?

Real estate investing is one of the best methods for building passive income. But for one to make a profitable income in real estate investments, it is important to know where and how you can find investment properties for sale that will produce a high return on investment. Being a real estate investor requires that you become resourceful, creative, and knowledgeable, so you need to know the different methods you can apply to find the best real estate properties.

There are different methods that investors can apply to find the best rental properties that are up for sale. By relying on a few resources, you provide yourself with the best chance to land the best investment.

Using networking to find a rental property

Not only is networking the best way to get profitable deals but also it offers a great opportunity to find rental properties that the general public may not know. Since not everyone knows about them, you have the chance to purchase these properties at a lower price. Important groups to the network include:

Personal investor network

This features a database of investors that you have been interacting with in the past few years, or you can start to keep from this time going forward. It can comprise of landlords whom you have interacted with or even old college friends who are now investors.

Investment clubs

Investment clubs are important contact because there is usually an email list where properties for sale are advertised or shared. If you haven't joined any clubs, it could be a great idea to join one. You can join a real estate investment club for a yearly membership fee between $100-$300.

Personal relationships

People in the real estate community aren't the only ones who can show you a great investment. Family, friends, and professional contacts can be great places to get possible investments. They could be experiencing a financial problem like a foreclosure, be aware of a person who knows of a property for sale. They may also have friends of their own who know important real estate investment opportunity. Your contractors can also be prospective sources to get leads because they can work for other investors that want to sell real estate.

Hire a real estate agent

Professionals exist to assist you with your investment. A real estate agent is a professional who knows exactly what to look out for in a property for sale. In addition, real estate agents access real estate resources that ordinary investors may not. Another way that a real estate agent can be helpful is connections. As you are aware, the real estate business involves networking with people. As a result, you cannot succeed without connections. An experienced real estate agent must have worked with different investors and other agents before. Therefore, he or she is supposed to assist you in finding rental properties for sale.

However, know that you may require to find a real estate agent who is experienced in matters to do with investment properties. Some agents may have worked with average homes, and that is a different story. It requires a professional to handle investment properties. Rental property investment deals require analysis of real estate property. From this analysis, you can determine the amount of return you can get on an investment property and select a profitable one.

Foreclosed properties

When thinking of how you can find rental investment properties, you should always remember to look at the local and national banks for foreclosed properties. Foreclosures, for example, make the best places for investment properties because they are sold at prices below the market value. Purchasing cheap rental properties lets real estate investors to attain a higher profit on every investment and can generate more money in real estate. And this is the purpose of every real estate investor.

Real estate open houses

You need to watch out for ads for real estate open houses in your local region and beyond. Real estate open houses are the best ways to find a property for sale instantly and to get an opportunity to ask any questions you may have before thinking of placing an offer on a property for sale.

Rental properties in print media

Print media is an effective method to find local listings. Some of these properties may not feature online, and so you will have little competition for them.

Newspapers

Newspapers are a handy source to get 'for sale by owner' properties plus Realtor listed on properties. You must ensure that you search for the main newspaper from your region, and other newspapers created for other specific cities.

Local marketing publications

You can get these smaller publications in most grocery stores. They are still a great place to land properties.

Auctions

Property auctions are another great place to find real estate deals. There are different types of auctions.

Online Auctions. You can look for investment on online auction websites like Auction.com.

Sherriff sale auctions: This type of auctions is done in the city hall of your county, courthouse, and hall of records. Foreclosures are first released to the general public at these sales. If no one buys the foreclosure at the auction, the foreclosing lender will own the property and list it as an REO using a local Realtor.

Private Auction Companies: For the private auction company, they are often contracted using lenders to sell a massive number of properties at a time. These auctions are advertised and conducted at a local hotel.

Finding rental properties using online tools and sources

Finding rental properties is something that many real estate investors have to Google search to get quick results that will provide answers to his or her predicament. No matter the kind of rental property that an investor shows interest in, they will at the one-point search for answers to this question.

However, this can be a bit difficult than it sounds. For example, if you type “rental properties around me,” it may generate thousands of search results to select from, with a few rental websites and firms offering the same service, and each having a different level of quality. In fact, it’s a big problem to find the best tool or website that will provide you with the best rental property.

But how can you select the best rental property online?

When searching for means to invest in real estate, the internet is one place where everyone turns to. As a result, the internet is the best place to turn to when looking for all types of rental properties. If you are looking for a house rental, then there is perhaps a rental website created to serve that specific function.

Some of the most popular searched words associated with real estate and finding investment rental properties include:

Condos for rent near me Foreclosures near me Townhomes near me

Typically, a few rental websites and companies have come up to solve these search phrases and offer homebuyers, and real estate investors with services and platforms that can be used to find any real estate property. Additionally, some rental companies and websites have focused entirely on specific types of real estate rental properties such as townhomes.

Despite this, real estate websites have increased in number in the last few years, and the reason is that many people are finding it hard to get real estate properties. As a result, the easiest channel to find rental properties is to look at online websites.

Types of house rental websites

While the main function of real estate websites is to help real estate investors and homebuyers to find rental properties, the tools, and services used by every website is different. Some rental websites offer more services than others.

Airbnb: This website is good for anyone looking for houses for rent for a short period. The invention of Airbnb resulted in an increase in the number of rental houses by personal homeowners. The idea behind Airbnb is to allow homeowners to become a landlord as long as they have an extra room or space that they think they can transform it into a rental house. The good side of this idea is that the homeowner earns a great profit from renting his or her house.

Nowadays, the hustle of finding a rental house is much easier than before because of the increase in the number of house rentals, and the development of rental websites that hook up investors.

There has also been the rise of rental property management companies that make work easier for real estate investors. The purpose of these companies is to manage the rental property on behalf of the investor, or homeowner. In this case, homeowners with rental far away from where they stay have no problem because everything is being taken care of.

For example, townhomes for rent have become popular places for real estate investors interested in rental properties. While these homes haven't been popular long-time ago, nowadays they have become a hot cake because of their remoteness and increased demand by travelers.

Other websites have entirely concentrated on renting out buildings and creating apartment finder tools to allow real estate investors to locate nearby apartments.

Using Mashvisor to find rental properties

Mashvisor was created to meet the needs of people, and to offer numerous services that can assist investors in finding houses for rentals. The site focuses on both traditional and Airbnb rental properties. It generates a long list of townhomes for rent, condos for rent, and other types of homes for rent. Whether you are looking for townhomes for rent near you or condos for rent around you, this site generates a detailed search result plus a map that will allow you to know the exact location.

CHAPTER 3

Flipping houses

The purpose of this chapter is to teach you more than a few steps you need to know to stay ahead of other house flippers. House flipping is a lucrative business, but you need to pay attention to detail to become successful.

Characteristics of a successful house flipper

Before you start to learn the steps, you need to follow to flip houses successfully, it is important to learn the traits of great house flippers. You can consider these as secrets of house flipping.

As long as you are committed, and dedicated, you will learn how to flip houses and generate profit. But as said before, you cannot purchase property without understanding the characteristics of successful house flippers. These are traits and skills that you must practice and apply if you want to make any profit and enjoy flipping houses.

Patience

Deals in house flipping run quickly when they start, but it takes time to land a deal that will earn a good profit. As a new house flipper, patience is critical in your daily operations because you will lose some money at the start, and slowly learn from your mistakes. The goal is to be patient and learn from every mistake you make, and then be ready to make some losses before you can get started.

Determination

A house flipper should be ready to learn something new for every house flip they make and then expand their network. You will also need to make all efforts to stay ahead of the competition all the time. You must show passion for house flipping to become successful because it will demand a great deal of your time to boost your business. Even when you succeed, you will still need to establish that intense edge to remain successful and expand your business.

Charismatic

If you didn't know, house flippers spend time in negotiation to land the best deal. As such, you must have a specific level of charisma to help you negotiate with lenders, buyers, contractors, and sellers. The main secret to developing the charisma is to become confident. Confidence arises from success. In other words, if you choose to master your trade and become the best flipper, then your confidence will start to show up when you negotiate deals.

Persistence

As a house flipper, there will be challenges that you will experience with your new project. Whenever these setbacks hit you, take a deep breath, look for a solution to the problem, and keep moving forward. As a new house flipper, you must know that you will encounter more than one challenge, and that should not make you give up on real estate business. To become successful in rental property investment, you must teach yourself to be persistent and fulfill your goals.

Let's now look at the Financial side of house flipping

One of the best things about this chapter is that you will learn everything that you need to know about house flipping. So at the end of the chapter, you will be ready to get started with house flipping. Keep in mind flipping houses isn't a get rich quick scheme, and it can make you lose all your capital if you aren't careful. It takes confidence and courage to launch a business in house flipping. Additionally, it demands great contacts for sources of funding and contractors.

Just like any other investment business, house flipping can eat all your money and leave you with nothing. This means if you get started with a poor plan, you may lose much more than what you input. If you select a house in a bad location and you fail to sell it immediately, then you could start to count losses right away. That is the reason why this chapter will take time to touch on every angle of house flipping that you must know before you can begin to flip your first house. This is done to avoid you making any losses while flipping houses.

One of the main reasons why a lot of people invest in real estate is because it can be a real gem once you get it right. Some house flippers boast of earning between $10, 000 -$100, 000 in profit on specific individual deals, and there are plenty of success stories of house flippers online. That is why it is advised that you look for a mentor who can present you with an actual account of their life story in house flipping including their failures. With house flipping, the odds for making a profit are huge, but you need to be always on alert to avoid making any losses.

House flipping rules that you must adhere to

In the whole of this chapter, we shall present you with a lot of rules that you must learn to assist you to attain success in flipping houses. When you stick to the rules of house flipping, you will realize that it's easier to get successful deals and buyers who will assist you in making a huge profit.

1. The more you spend, the more you should generate

If you decide to pump $40, 000 to renovate a home that will earn you $20, 000 profit, then this is not a great deal that you should involve yourself. Large renovation projects are done to generate big profits, and this is a rule that you must not forget whenever you want to purchase a distressed property.

2. Don't take on more than you can handle

For new investors, the first successful flip can create more expectations than expected. As a result, the investor ends up taking up a lot of projects, or even participate in projects that are beyond their potential. As said before, this is not a get-rich pyramid scheme. Instead, it is an investment where you develop on your experience by working on projects that you can handle and maintain your workload to an amount that you can successfully track all the time.

3. Don't leave anything to chance

You will go through a lot of information associated with planning your flip so that you don't get any surprise but only make a profit. The advantage of planning every aspect of your flip cannot be underrated. Once you gain some bit of experience, you will discover that the plans you set up for your flip will turn out to be the best path to success.

4. Always look for good advice

After spending a few years flipping houses, you will become confident while working on certain areas of your projects. But still, the most successful house flippers usually look for reliable advice from professionals to help them boost their knowledge base. Successful flippers don't think that they have all the answers because arrogance breeds losses.

5. Trust yourself

If you adhere to every step-by-step advice provided in this chapter and make it a habit to check and re-check your information, then you will acquire the confidence to trust every decision you make. You might start by making guesses, but the experience will help you to trust your instincts over time.

Knowing the fear you will feel

There's so much to say about the power of positive thinking when you flip homes. Real estate investing isn't a business for those with a weak heart, you must be committed and confident of seeing projects until the end. If you want to involve yourself in house flipping, then you must know how to manage the mental setbacks that will always pop-up in the process. The first emotion you will need to deal with is fear, and it can take some time before you get in the right mental state to conquer the feat that comes with house flipping.

Fear itself

The single important reason why people ditch their dreams of house flipping is fear. And fear is the main factor that prevents people from fulfilling their potential. The first thing that happens to your subconscious mind when you take a look at house flipping is to challenge your motivations and worry related to the possible outcomes. Fear is that type of hesitation that will cause you to stop and begin to ask yourself questions. That is the reason why being educated about house flipping is critical.

You are probably reading this because you have made up your mind on a decision that is causing fear inside your heart, or you want to discover more about house flipping and assess whether the fear you have is true. It is normal to challenge yourself or doubt yourself when you want to flip houses, but it is crucial that you eliminate that fear if you want to become successful. So, let's start by finding out the different types of fear that may arise when you get started with house flipping.

Common Fears

Simply because something is known all over doesn't mean it is understood. You may identify all the types of fears involved in house flipping, but we shall assist you to overcome those fears and get on the track of making money.

The house fails to sell

Each fear related with house flipping can be overcome with effective planning. Many new house flippers fear that a house may fail to sell, so they disregard the investment. In the whole of this chapter, you will learn exactly how to recognize homes that can sell quickly.

This chapter will also teach you on steps to take to sell your property fast at a reduced profit and means to make money with your property while still on the market. Even if your house doesn't sell immediately, you will still have numerous options to make a profit.

Running low of cash

Nothing is so frustrating than a house flipper running low of cash before completing the first project. The right way you fund a house flipping project is to plan your remodeling money, purchase money, and to hold costs in the bank. You should not over-plan your house flip when you collect all your funds together.

When you gather your remodeling budget, make sure that you set aside around 20 percent to deal with unforeseen circumstances. If you aren't sure about your abilities to define the needs to be done for a successful house remodeling, then it's better to look for a professional. Once you hire a professional to assist you in planning your remodeling project, then you will save some money in the end.

Holding costs refer to monthly bills that you pay as the property owner, such as utilities, mortgage payments, and maintenance. When you organize your house flip, ensure that you also set aside three months of holding costs in your budget. So if the house doesn't sell after three months, then you should sell it to a wholesaler or rent it out for a fixed amount. You have choices when it comes to money, so you should not be worried about running out.

Lose cash on the deal

So far you have learned something on how to eliminate the fear of losing money on a flip, but there are some tips on how you can eliminate that fear for good.

Add 20 percent to the numbers you develop for your flip budget steps (purchase, remodeling, and holding). If you are working on a budget with the purchase price, then you will have some extra to channel to the remodeling project and holding expenses.

Keep in mind that landing some funding from a lender and outlining the property via a real estate agent may also have costs related to them. Don't forget to put the costs in your budget.

If you are unsure how correctly estimate the value of a home, then register for a real estate course. The investment will assist you in estimating the values of property and avoiding overpaying.

If you decide to purchase properties using foreclosure auctions, keep in mind that you will often not be allowed to look at the interior of the property before you can place a bid. Foreclosures can be a gold mine if you really know whatever you are doing, but you might want to look at various auctions that happen before you place bid yourself.

There is nothing like too much planning for a house flip. If you plan to eliminate the fear of losing money, then you should ensure that you learn everything you can relate to housing flipping before you begin and continue to learn every day. Always make the necessary plans on every project, and make arrangements as possible. There are no secrets to success in house flipping, so don't look for the easiest ways.

The fear of setbacks to remodeling

Some people see a house in a remodeling stage and decide to destroy it. Others see a construction site and think like they have to steal everything that is not nailed down.

Your worries in remodeling can also stretch to other activities that you cannot regulate. If you find a stretch of bad weather, then you may need to close it down. If a person forgets to file for the permission rights, then the city or town you are in will close down. You need not fear such unknown contingencies since you will always be ready for them.

Insurance: You need to make your house flipping business professional by integrating or at least completing a business certificate, and next insure your operations. You can speak to a commercial insurance sales professional about insurance to safeguard against theft, lost revenue, bad weather, and anything that you think of. Don't start a house flipping business without the correct insurance in place.

Great communication: If your remodeling worksite supervisor is permitted to stop work because of insufficient permission, then it is important for the supervisor to know how to strike a hold immediately so that the problem is solved. Effective communication between contractors, real estate agents, and investors can solve most flipping challenges.

Emergency funding: Suppose you want to stop a task just because you underestimated remodeling funding? If you own the credit lines, and other funding plans in place, then this should never be a big issue.

Fear should never prevent you from flipping houses because you can clear all fears using great research and detailed planning. When you decide to flip houses, your next step should be to combine the resources to start. The entrepreneur who expects success should never allow fear to get in the way to attaining a profit.

In the next part, you will learn more about how to handle all of your fears related to house flipping. You will go through comprehensive info to teach you how to change from being a hesitant investor to a brave entrepreneur.

Overcoming the fear of flipping

Once you know the fears associated with house flipping and the way those fears build, the next thing is to overcome those fears and start working. As said before, you must have a detailed knowledge of house flipping before you can eliminate your hesitations and begin investing. Once you get started, the experience that you acquire will assist you in setting aside all fears and becoming aggressive and successful flipper.

Always develop a plan

It is said that having a plan in place will assist you in handling your fears, but what does that imply? Combining a plan for house flipping will work as a guide and assist you to avoid making costly mistakes. When you are a newbie to house flipping, it is hard to recall everything you need to ensure that a flip is successful. Your plan can work like a checklist that ensures you remain on track. The parts of a great house flipping plan comprise:

Selling prices- If you want to take part in neighborhoods that tend to sell properties at a profit, then you will require different online resources to identify the types of properties that appreciate in value in specific neighborhoods.

Selling out great Properties-A great neighborhood is but just half of the equation when it comes to generating profit while flipping. You must take time to comprehensively scan out every property in a neighborhood, and only handle properties that have a lot of room for making a profit. Purchasing a property that isn't distressed and selling at a close to retail will not allow you to generate profit. Keep in mind that simply because you remodel a property doesn't imply it will sell for the profit you want.

Neighborhood dynamics- Select neighborhoods with properties that sell fast. If you pick on a neighborhood that has a history of properties that stay on the market for over six months, then you will find it difficult to generate profit in that field.

Be great with numbers

House flipping requires that you are good working with numbers. You must know how to determine remodeling costs, know how profit is generated, and recognize when a deal is realistic. If you aren't well of with math, then you must set aside time to attend classes to boost your math skills. Experience working in a crunching real estate number will finally make you an expert in generating accurate computations, and you must always be open to new methods for applying figures you generate.

Every house flipping transaction has a pattern, and that pattern is:

Identify the amount of profit you want to generate before you participate in any property deals. Be alert in combining comprehensive figures that will make up for each aspect of the flip.

Maintain reliable notes on each mathematics feature involved in transactions.

Don't fear to consult with a professional if your numbers don't work out, or you aren't sure what you can do with the numbers.

Don't flip on your own

Many flippers avoid involving financial partners because they don't want to share any profit. That is a great entrepreneurial attitude, but it doesn't imply that you need to run your flipping business on your own. In the business sector, the most successful people know that they don't know everything and they ask for help from other people.

Real estate investors Association-There is an REIA group around you, and you must join it and stay as active as possible. Every member in an REIA takes part in meetings for the same reasons; to network with other investors and extend their opportunities. Certain REIA members are always happy to describe parts of the process you may not know, while others prefer to exchange information for the opportunity. If you would like to flip a house successfully, then you must be an active member of your local REIA.

Get a mentor- When you participate in REIA meetings or any other professional networking task, you will begin to speak to people who have attained a certain level of success that you would like to attain. When these people are ready to guide you, and show you the correct path to take, they become your mentors. When it comes to house flipping, nothing is more important than being able to make a phone call and get advice from a professional expert.

Online mentors- These refer to house flipping experts who reach to a large online audience, and they can assist you to boost your profitability. The challenge with online mentors is that many people want to scam entrepreneurs instead of giving them good advice. If you choose to acquire information from an online mentor, be on the lookout for people who ask huge amounts of cash for industry advice.

Try a partner- If you are getting started with house flipping, then it may be a good thing to try a joint project with an expert flipper for your first few projects. You may learn a great deal about the details required in house flipping when you become part of a partnership.

Give yourself a learning curve

Fear can always lead to frustration if you don't allow yourself to learn as you move along. Take every flipping project slowly, and realize that you will make mistakes in the first few projects. The secret is to learn from those mistakes and not to get angry at yourself for committing them. If you use your mistakes to improve your knowledge, then you will become a better flipper as time goes by.

What you only need to fear is?

When you are starting a new business that you aren't familiar with, fear is inevitable. The two steps that you need to deal with fear are recognizing that which scares you and then building a detailed plan to overcome the worries. For house flipping, the greatest fear that engulfs many new house flippers is the fear to lose all their money.

One thing that results in early anxiety on the side of the house flipper is the feeling that they are in over their heads. However, with the correct mentors and a strong partner to assist you in starting, you can learn as you proceed without leading to your business collapsing. The next thing to recall is that you will fail more than once when you get started. If you are aware that failure is coming, then you must use it to your advantage rather than fearing it. People who have made it in life learn from their mistakes, and apply confidence to get ready to conquer fear.

Building your investment criteria

The concept of planning for each house flip cannot be underrated as planning is the most step of any successful business. When looking for the correct properties, you must have an outline that you need to follow that will assist you in choosing the best investments. Although it is true that you are expecting, until the time you begin remodeling, you can highly boost your opportunities of generating profit by rapidly using the experience to improve your investment procedure.

The important elements of a great flip

In this section, you will benefit a lot by learning the important elements that you must consider to decide on whether or not to pursue an investment opportunity. Before you start to process any real numbers or involve contractors to develop estimates, you must identify whether the type of property you want has all the features of a great flip.

The correct location- The location of the property will define its value and the speed at which it will sell. If you want to get properties located in the neighborhoods where homes sell quickly, and home values appreciate fast. Do some research on the type of neighborhoods said to be the best to invest in and eliminate neighborhoods that pose challenges to your business.

A great foundation- As a house flipper, you must be ready to replace some drywall and perform roof repairs. However, you need a house that is structurally well and sits on a great foundation. Mold, damage to wooden house frame, and cracked foundation walls are red flags that you want to clear out.

A better school district-A house located in a school district with a characteristic for providing safe and effective schools will sell much faster.

The potential of a value- When house flipper spots a problem in an old home, they see the opportunity to make money. Homes lose value because of many things that are easy to correct. When you look at properties to flip, aim to pay the least possible for a house that can generate a strong profit.

Pay attention to market Trends-Market trends in rental business differ from one neighborhood to the next. You may come across a great neighborhood, but the recent houses for sale have stayed for months. Examine trends for every market and only choose to invest in neighborhoods that reflect an upward trend in home pricing.

Analyze your profit

The profit you generate will not always be the profit you want, but you must define a profit as part of your plan to house flipping. There are two methods to determine your possible profit:

As a set amount

As a function of remodeling costs

Many flippers determine profit based on a function of remodeling costs because it is an easier alternative to perform things. Let's imagine that you bought a foreclosed property for about $45,000. The retail value of the same property is $125,

000 and you think it will require around $35,000 to repair it. You estimate that it will require about three months to sell, so you factor in an extra $1,250 for different holding costs and transaction fees.

Your total investment would be around $83,750, and you approximate that it will sell for $120,000. This generates a possible profit of $36, 250, which may be a little more or less based on how quickly the property sells. Keep in mind that your remodeling costs may include a pad of 20 percent to take care of any unforeseen costs.

Now, suppose in this case, you choose to make $38,000 in return? When you decide to make a lump sum profit number, you must regulate all the numbers around it to ensure that it works. If it is hard to change the selling price, then you need to return to the remodeling plan and attempt to reduce the costs. Be keen when you choose to reduce the remodeling costs because those reductions will prevent you from selling the property fast enough to generate profit.

Another method to make a large profit is to buy the property as a distressed property and sell it to a wholesaler at a constant price. The wholesaler will want to sell the property to another flipper, so you may require to lower your profit expectations. However, when you want to make a quick profit on flipping a house, then using a wholesaler is the best path to take.

For you to attain your massive profit, you may need to consider getting a tenant while the house is still for sale. While this may be a bit hard to get a tenant who wants to sign a three-month lease, you can think about renting the property for a year and let the value of the property appreciate to attain a huge profit. Your tenant will handle your holding costs, and you may increase your profit by letting the property appreciate.

Holding expenses and fees

Holding costs refer to the expenses you pay at the end of the month to keep and maintain the property you sell. It is impossible to show a house unless it has the power turned on, and someone has to maintain the landscaping to keep the appeal. Monthly holding costs comprise:

Repair costs- When something happens to the property, such as vandalism or break-in, then you may need to assume the financial responsibility for performing the repairs. This is the point where another holding cost, homeowners' insurance, can become handy.

Maintenance Costs-Regardless of whether you decide to perform the maintenance yourself or hire someone, there shall be costs involved.

Utilities.

Homeowner's association Fees-You may have to think twice about attempting to flip a house in a gated community or any place that has association fees.

Mortgage payments-If you financed your property buying, then you will require a monthly payment to make sure that the property remains in your name. You may also need to pay monthly payments on any loans you take to perform the remodeling, and you will need to pay the related loan fees each month.

Many new flippers don't consider the long list of fees that occurs with flipping a house. Those fees comprise of:

Property Taxes-You will be accountable for paying the prorated property taxes when you sell the property.

Closing Costs-You may decide to shift your closing costs into your financing when you purchase the property, or you may pay them up front. These comprise of property surveys, insurance costs, legal costs, and title search costs.

Liens- In case there are liens on the property that the owner doesn't want to pay, then you may have to pay for them before the purchase can pass.

Code violations-In the remodeling process, you may compile a few code violations that must be paid before you can sell the property.

As you get ready to invest in house flipping, you must have a blueprint to notify you of the massive financial duties that are involved in house flipping. A written guide can act as a template to build a comprehensive budget, and your best method to avoid losing any money on a flip. Profit isn't guaranteed, but people who decide to plan these things out are meant to be successful.

Finding homes to flip

If you are a savvy real estate investor, finding great properties to flip is important as the flip itself. When looking for a great property to flip, your main goal is to find a distressed property or distressed owners. You will learn more about a distressed property, or owner, but the idea is that you want don't want to purchase properties that require a retail price and should perhaps get it.

House flipping is a business that needs a person to stay patient because you will have to consider at least three, or four options for each decision you make. You need to speak to different lenders, attorneys, or contractors before you choose on who to hire, and you need to do your due diligence when looking for properties. Although you may need to look for more than one house to flip at a time, you need to always factor at least three or four properties to offer yourself different options to select from.

What should you look for?

Before you can look for properties to flip, you must have a great idea as to what you are targeting. A distressed property refers to one that requires repair before it is sold for retail value. Many distress properties are abandoned for some time, which makes the negotiation of a purchase a bit easier. A distressed owner is one that is about to enter into foreclosure, or has experienced life changes that demand to sell their home a necessity.

Below is a list of various conditions that result in a distressed house and owners. Most of the information that you need to find these kinds of properties is available online.

Houses hit with the building code or zoning law violations.

Owners that have been forced to leave town and are desperate to sell their houses quickly. Homes listed as being in pre-foreclosure because of various missed consecutive payments.

Couples who have filed for marriage divorce and may be interested in selling their house at a discount. Get in touch with families of the recently deceased to assist them in selling their loved one's home fast. People convicted of a crime, or lost a major civil lawsuit, and cannot afford their homes at all.

Members of the military who are about to be deployed and might want to sell their home before they leave. Going to attend foreclosure auctions and placing bids.

Replying to classified ads for people who are selling distressed homes, and putting your classified ad in a local newspaper ready to purchase distressed homes.

Take advantage of online resources to get sellers of distressed properties and potential buyers if you want to sell a home without remodeling.

Go driving and look out for distressed properties in a specific area. The contact details of the owner should be in a file at a city hall in case the home is abandoned.

Learning more about foreclosure auctions

Before you can begin to place bids at foreclosure auctions, it is good to attend some and look at the way the process takes place. At an auction, you are not always given any additional time to take a look at how the property appears, and you won't be allowed to get inside. Therefore, if you know the address of the auction early, then you can attempt to take a glance of the property in advance, but still, you won't be permitted to get inside.

It is crucial that you are aware of the procedure of an auction before you decide to participate, or else your bid may get you in a huge hole that is hard to come out. Some auctions may need you to pay cash at the end, while others will allow you to have funding organized that would feature short term payments. Either way, you should be ready to pay for the foreclosed property the day you purchase it, and you may be requested to pay back taxes and any liens that are on the property too.

Innovative methods to find properties

Sometimes, it requires a person to go beyond the normal to get properties to flip. Part of the joy of flipping a house is building new methods to identify properties and see the same properties generate profits.

Search through a Multiple Listing Service (MLS) expired listings to get properties that are still on the market. In some instances, the owners may be ready to sell the property at a discount just to eliminate it.

Many banks have a Real Estate Owned (REO) department that produces lists of properties that emerge for foreclosure. Get in touch with banks and begin to request for their REO foreclosure lists.

Search for current MLS listings for properties that feature a large number of Days on Market (DOM) time. You may need to research your market to learn the way DOM time is too much, but the best rule of thumb is to get in touch with owners that have properties featured on the list for over a year.

When you investigate the MLS listings in your place, ensure that you get in touch with owners with listings that passed through different price changes.

Other possible property owners that you may work with are people who have recently closed down their business, people who have retired recently, and would like to sell their home to purchase a smaller one and any other situation where a property may be distressed.

Getting in touch with owners

Flipping homes is a mathematical game, and that means that you need to try and reach out to most distressed property owners as possible. One way to achieve this is by purchasing a mailing list depending on the criteria outlined, and then send out postcards to every owner who offers you their service.

Another great way to contact many distressed owners of distressed properties is to build a working association with many real estate agents as possible. You can provide agents with a finder's fee once a property is flipped; this implies that you would only pay as an agent for a property that is sold at a profit. Real estate agents can also be invaluable resources for getting buyers once a remodeling project is complete.

If you want to succeed in house flipping, then you must know the type of properties that will make the best inventory. Unless you have sufficient financial resources, it is better to keep your flipping projects to one or two at a time. Once you get going, you will find it difficult to turn deals down. But with time, you will build the experience and professional network that you require to turn every type of distressed property into a lucrative deal.

Finding and rehabbing a home

It requires time before an investor can find and purchase properties that make the best flipping projects. Every investor has their own means of doing things, and the best investors let their skills evolve as they gain confidence in their strength to spot the best deals. But regardless of great an investor becomes at recognizing deals, there are sections of the search and rehab procedure that cannot be reversed. If it is not broken, then don't try to fix it, and if you begin generating money by depending on the expertise of other people, then you must learn to take the professional advice into account.

Assessing the property

First, the investor has to become satisfied that the property can generate profit once it is rehabbed before anything else takes place. With time, most house flippers start to trust their guts when it comes to purchasing or walking away from specific properties. The more experience you get as time goes, the more refined your instincts become. But most importantly, the experience will direct you on what specifically to look out in a property that will make it a success.

Most of the properties an investor purchases to flip are sold via auctions where is no chance to look at the property over to recognize whether it is a great deal. Given that a house a flipper can make a good size of their money assessing auction properties, it is sensible to spend time building the skills required to assess properties fast. Some investors are so good at finding out what they can bid on an auction just using the pictures offered.

For those properties that an investor has the opportunity to look around and examine the deal, it is a great thing to involve a professional contractor. As a house flipper, you will become better at highlighting details that could either make or break deals, but you can never the eye of an experienced contractor. You can learn a lot by assessing properties with a contractor and pumping some cash to bring a contractor along can prevent you from making significant losses if you attempt to flip a property that may not deliver profit.

Getting the best contractor

If you want to build a career from house flipping, then you don't need a great contractor to work with you. What you need is the right contractor for you and your business. This requires a contractor that you can trust, and has the best interests in mind, is ready to work with you on flipping projects, and probably one who has several crews that can get various projects done simultaneously.

Every successful flipper has at least one contractor whom they work with often to recognize opportunities and have projects finished on time. Your contractor will know the way you want to run your business when they can take time and make decisions on your behalf, and how you are prepared to save money on the remodeling budget. It is possible to go for short cuts on a remodeling project and still attain great results; the goal is to get a contractor who is aware of building codes and materials so good that they can make replacements that receive quality results for lower prices.

Spend some time at the Home Depot

If you visit the Home Depot every weekday morning, you will see local contractors picking up supplies, purchase new equipment, and swap information with other contractors around the area. The Home Depot even simplifies the process of getting contractors by having a different loading area for contractors and their materials.

Therefore, if you are searching for a great contractor, then the Home Depot is a great place to hang out for a few weeks and watch out the contractors who often appear to purchase materials. A contractor who just comes once or twice a week is perhaps not going to be interested or even take on a flipping investor. However, those who show up every day at Home Depot are great contractors who want to take on a steady client.

Speak to other investors

It may not be easy to find trade secrets from successful house flippers, but it doesn't hurt to try. While you participate in house flipping, you will begin to meet the same people at auctions and some at distressed properties you believe you found on your own. Some of the investors could be interested in mentor new flippers while others may be tight-lipped.

Ensure that you make yourself available to other flippers around to receive referrals for great contractors. You join with professional flippers for deals and discover who you can speak to for great advice on properties. A savvy flipper may discover methods to get others to trust them and find the information they need to remain successful.

Become a member of the Real Estate Investors Association

There are plenty of reasons to take part in your local chapter of the Real Estate Investors Association (REIA), and getting the best contractor is one of them. An REIA meeting is a great place where you can start to network with different experts who can simplify your life. Contractors that want to work with house flippers often attend these meetings, and they are ready to meet you.

Regardless of where you get your contractor referrals from, you must take time to examine each referral and only do business with contractors who fulfill your guidelines. You need to recruit experienced professionals who have a reliable and mature direction to the business. After all, the type of contractor you choose to work with will have great input on the way you make decisions, and you want to be confident that you have selected the correct person to work with.

Handling your remodeling project

You get a reliable contractor to perform the remodeling projects because you need it done in the right way, but you will still require to manage the projects on your end to ensure that every project produces a profit.

Ensure you watch out on your costs and never fear to ask your contractor on the money they are spending. In case there are cost-effective means to find results, then you need to emphasize on those methods. If your contractor challenges a problem that will need more money to solve, then you should discuss all your options before making the final decision.

Have a separate contract with your contractor for each project, and there should be penalty clauses for missed deadlines. There is no problem with holding your contractor accountable for spending your money. But to ensure that your contractor defines the project deadlines. It is not good for you to set deadlines that are hard to be attained, but you can learn to agree on deadlines that are discussed with your contractor. If your contractor fails to fulfill a deadline, then you can look at the liquidated damages. This is the figure, often $100 per day, that you reduce from the final price of the project for every day it is late.

Spend part of your time to research on ways you can make improvements that add value to a home. For example, improving the technology of home and adding technological changes. You can still add value by building solar panels on a home to help reduce energy costs. In some instances, remodeling the bathroom will also generate value, but you need to know when these improvements will be effective and when they are not worth it.

Improving the appeal is one of the most critical factors in selling a property fast and for more money. You need to concentrate on landscaping and exterior changes that will draw the attention of people as they come close to the home.

The odds of landing a great flipping project and get it repaired quickly is important to your success as a house flipper. You have to spend a lot of time learning how to recognize the best deals and networking with industry experts who can assist you in making the best decisions.

Approximating repair costs on your flip

This section is focused entirely on repair and remodeling costs because of the role it plays in creating a complete price. It is hard to estimate the amount you need to offer to purchase a distressed property until you learn how much profit you can make. Both your repair and remodeling estimate is part of your general investment cost which also involves the purchase price of the property and holding costs. It is important that each flipper understand how to approximate remodeling costs, or repair costs, even if they plan to look for a contractor to estimate for them.

Why should you know how to estimate repair costs?

As your flipping business continues to grow you will discover two critical lessons:

If you decide to wait before you pull off a deal, then you are probably going to lose the deal.

Contractors work based on their schedules and don't have that time to come with you to build a comprehensive approximation.

When you don't want to estimate or make remodeling estimates on your own for your first few deals, it can affect your business. Therefore, you must try your best to learn so that your business doesn't stop because you cannot perform an estimate of repair or remodeling costs. The best deal for a distressed property may emerge on a Tuesday morning and disappear by evening. If you are relying on your contractor to perform the estimates, then you will find it hard to take advantage of the deals that you come across.

The reason for repairing and remodeling a property

Some real estate investors look for distressed properties at low prices and then flip the same properties as fast as they can. In such a business, one must learn how to deal with the highest deals if the aim is to make any substantial profit. A quick turnaround deal on the distressed property may generate in $2, 000 or $3, 0000 in profit. However, in case you remodel the property, you may see profits in the tens of thousands of dollars.

Your reputation plays a huge role when it comes to real estate investing, and having a reputation of being a high- volume distressed property buyer and seller is going to reduce your chances. Individuals who hold onto top deals often want to see something done with the property to change the neighborhood. If your goal is to purchase and sell distressed properties quickly, then you will realize that you have to create your own deals always. When you become popular as a person who utilizes distressed properties, then your phone will ring every time.

Your intention as a real estate investor is to generate profit, and the best method to make a profit is to remodel or even repair the property to ensure that it suits with the remaining completed sections in the neighborhood. Purchasing distressed property at a low price, and selling it as close to retail is the best strategy to build a successful real estate investing business.

Renovation to scale

Is it sensible to spend more money to change a property into a million-dollar showpiece in a neighborhood where the average property is estimated at $200, 000? Well, as a house flipper, you must learn to work in different areas where the value of a property comes at different levels. If you attempt to do a lot to a property, you may price it out of the market, and you may lose a lot of cash. However, losing money isn't the only way of overdoing in remodeling a house.

Your million-dollar house sitting in a $200, 000 neighborhoods may devalue the properties around it, and that may build a bad association with the homeowners in the neighborhood. At the very least, if you decide to put a highly priced property around a place with average properties, that may result in a reassessment of all the properties in that area, and thus destroy your association with other homeowners.

By overdoing it when it comes to remodeling may result in a property to stay unsold until the time you reduce the costs to avoid losing everything. People who want to purchase homes in a given neighborhood often don't want to pay more than the per house average for that particular area. Your high-priced rehab may have a difficult time to attract prospective buyers, and it may be the last project your company ever does.

The neighborhood can be your biggest friends in selling your remodeled property if you ensure that the property is in the correct price range. Homeowners hate to see abandoned properties in their neighborhoods because it hurts the property value of everyone. You could be that neighborhood's hero if you perform the correct remodeling project and change an abandoned property into a great part of the community.

Look for detail

As you work together with your contractor on setting prices on the first few rehab projects, build a checklist of things a contractor should focus and fill that list for each project. Some of the best parts of a home when it comes to remodeling estimates that people miss comprising:

The foundation

The electrical wiring Pests and insects The plumbing

The sewage system

As time goes by, you will come up with a detailed checklist that will allow you to perform your own inspections and determine the type of work that requires to be done. Your contractor will also speak in terms of costs per square feet for showing how much the work will cost. Once you look at this technique, you need to be able to apply it to your own estimates with the right degree of accuracy.

Other aspects new investors fail to consider include the title search and land survey. In many cases, any problem with the survey and the title search can be dealt with easily. However, there are times when some remodeling may fix the title or the survey, and you may need to highlight those problems and develop solutions.

Putting in the notebook

As a real estate investor, you must have two assumptions about your remodeling estimate, or the estimate you receive from the contractor, to eliminate any problem.

The project will surpass the budget

The project will take longer than expected

Although you may have the regular project that clocks in on time and on budget, you must plan for the worst situation. That is the reason why you need to add an extra of 20 percent both on the budget and the timetable. You need to include this additional percent on your own approximations and estimates you acquire from contractors. The added percent is one that you use to define the amount of money you can generate from every deal.

A great house flipper understands how to take advantage of the available resources to them, but they still know that the best deal waits for nobody. New flippers should stay clear of combining their remodeling estimates unless they have some knowledge about the general contracting. But with time, an experienced flipper should gain the correct skills required to build their own estimates and utilize the best deals when they arise.

Purchasing a distressed property

Once you have built up your network of sellers and have selected a distressed property you want to purchase, the next thing is to come up with a good offer that will win you a house. When it comes to house flipping, it is hard to get a second chance at putting an offer on the same distressed property. Thus, you must learn how to build a compelling first offer, and from there negotiate with the seller until the property becomes yours.

In most cases, the seller of distressed property is only going to sell the property as fast as possible at some profit. Wholesalers will identify the type of property they want to make, but there is always a chance for negotiation. Homeowners are always interested in selling fast than generating a massive profit, but you cannot handle homeowners the way you do with wholesalers.

For a real estate deal to succeed, all parties have to feel like they are getting the best deal. Obviously, you want to acquire property for the least price possible, but you need to know that the seller has to make a profit too. Negotiating in good faith is often going to get you further than constant aggressive negotiations.

Coming up with your initial offer

Before you choose to make an initial offer on a property, you must decide on whether the deal will work for you. You can do that by:

Deciding on the retail value of the property once you remodel by analyzing similar properties in the area. Approximate remodeling costs, liens, taxes, and holding costs.

Identify the buying price, holding costs, remodeling costs to find After Repair Value (ARV).

Remove the ARV from the retail value, and that will generate the profit you need to make.

You can avoid taking part in wrong deals by taking away 20 percent from your profit estimate to get a conservative number that you can work with. In case the numbers work on your side, then it will be time to create an offer to the homeowner.

You can change the possible profit to get either a lower or higher offer, but you cannot adjust your remodeling costs. Once you adjust the numbers and feel okay with the initial offer you have developed, then you can send the offer to the owner.

Get in touch with contingencies

When both of you and the seller reach an agreement on a given price, you should move on to put that price in writing and include plans to protect yourself. What can you do in case you don't get financing? The easiest method is to protect yourself is to involve stipulations within the contract that define the completion of the deal is contingent once:

Financing is approved A clean inspection

An agreeable appraisal

You need to also include a specific time frame for the contingencies of 30 days. If nothing takes place within 30 days of the initial agreement, then the deal is off. This will offer you the time to get all your inspections and appraisals in one place, and it is also securing you from a seller who may try to shop your price to other buyers.

Make sure that the contract defines the property as being sold "as-is" depending on the status when you agreed to the price. This will secure you from any destruction that might happen to the property and makes the owner accountable for maintaining the condition of the property in which you initially saw it.

Once you agree to a price, then you can put a deposit on the contract to ensure that the property remains there in your name. Make sure that the contingency is in the contract that requires you to get your deposit back once the deal falls through.

CHAPTER 4

Property Wholesaling

Real estate wholesaling is one of the best real estate investment methods. But for one to succeed in this business, it is important to know the little details involved in property wholesaling. So, in this section, we take you through everything that you need to know about real estate wholesaling.

But before we dive into details, you need to understand what property wholesaling means. When we talk about property wholesaling, it implies that your role is that of a middleman. You meet a motivated seller, negotiate the property for a specific low price, and then resell it for a low price but higher than the purchasing price. The differences between the two prices are your profit.

For example:

You meet an ambitious seller who wants to sell his property instantly. The first thing you need to do is to negotiate the price. It is easy to find motivated sellers because of life circumstances that they may have experienced such as foreclosure. This creates the opportunity to get the property at a much lower price. Now that you have an agreement with the property owner concerning the price move forward and allocate the property to a contract. This particular contract shall have a date by which you must get an end-buyer for the home. You begin searching for a real estate investor who is interested in purchasing investment properties for a very low price. Lastly, you close the deal with the end buyer.

Now you could be asking yourself about the money part. Well, this section comes between the negotiation with the property seller and closing the deal with the end-buyer. For instance, if you have an agreement with the seller on

$50,000 as the price of the home. Then you get a real estate investor who is ready to purchase the property for around $70, 000. The $20, 000 difference is what you pocket in from the deal. This is how you make money in real estate via wholesaling.

What is the best way to make money via real estate wholesaling?

Real estate wholesaling is one of the best methods to earn money in real estate. But the amount of money you generate depends on the size of your clients. What this means is that deciding to wholesale investment properties may be a better choice than residential properties. The reason is simple; there is always a real estate investor out there who is ready to purchase investment properties. It is simple for you to discover an end-buyer who would like to invest in property instead of living in it. Real estate investors are always searching for the best deals in the real estate sector, and in this case, you possess what they want. As a result, focusing on a specific category of clients may be a great strategy to generate money in real estate.

Well, how is real estate wholesaling different from house flipping?

Real estate property wholesaling is similar to the fix-and-flip strategy. In both methods, you acquire a property for a low price and then later resell it. Still, there are two major differences:

Fixing the property: As the name goes, it involves fixing and flipping the property. In other words, you purchase a property for a low price because of the distressed state. You make the necessary repairs and then resell it to a different person for a much higher price. This is related to forced appreciation. Once you apply the changes to the property, it increases in value so you can generate profit.

On the other hand, if you wholesale property, you don't do any repairs. You also don't purchase the property. You agree to a price and look for an end-buyer who will implement all the necessary changes.

Regardless of the direction, it doesn't imply that you will earn an extremely damaged home. In certain cases, the damages may only cost a few hundred dollars.

The return on investment: The main goal of wholesaler is to make money in real estate. When it comes to real estate investing, it is referred to as return on investment. With property wholesaling, you will be investing a few hundred dollars and your chance to acquire a high rate of return on what you have invested. But for fix and flip, you invest more time and money in remodeling the house. This doesn't imply that you don't get a great profit on your investment. It only implies that you invest a lot.

Why is property wholesaling popular?

As a real estate wholesaler, your task is to look for people interested in the property and assist the property owner in supporting the sale. Your role is not to market the property. When you adhere to these rules, you can make transactions that will not make you lose your money.

With real estate wholesaling, there is no need to put any money down, and there is nothing to lose if you cannot get an interested buyer for the home. Keep in mind that the contract expires once you fail to get a buyer. If you let a lot of contracts to expire, then your track record is ruined. However, if you work extremely hard and study the business, you can become a great expert at uniting buyers and sellers in the low-risk business.

Basic concepts of wholesaling

This section will focus on the basic elements you must have before you can start wholesaling properties. That includes:

Approaching the seller- There is a correct way and wrong way to introduce your services and yourself to a property owner.

Math and Negotiations-You must be good working with numbers in wholesaling, and you need to understand how to use the same numbers to come up with the best deal.

Get in touch with the owner of Property-There are various ways to create wholesaling contracts that you must know.

Presenting the Deal-You will learn the best ways to land lucrative deals and the way to present your real estate deal.

Legality

You have made the first step towards real estate property wholesaling by reading this chapter. Now is time to dive deep into the world of wholesaling and demonstrate to you how you can get started.

For you to expand your network of sellers with your real estate wholesaling business, you must look for methods to reach out to people who may be interested in your services. As long as you regularly update your details, respond to your metrics, and continue to collect new information, you will find the sellers to speak to.

There are different methods you can use to market your business services to a specific audience, but one of the most effective methods is direct mail marketing. This particular marketing requires generation and mailing of physical flyers and data sheets to possible sellers to develop an interest in your business.

Why is direct mail the best?

There are a few reasons as to why successful property wholesalers prefer direct mail. First, a wholesaler who regularly updates their direct mail contact will build a list that contains names of people who want to sell their homes. Direct mail eliminates the guess away from marketing and allows you to talk directly to your audience.

It can be quite difficult for individuals who depend on technology to understand the power of paper. When a buyer visits a property you want to sell holding your flyer on their hands, then you can recognize how powerful direct mail can be. A marketing piece relays a single message, and on a piece of paper. This message is not diluted with pop-up ads and thousands of other irrelevant digital marketing.

Tips to creating a great direct mail campaign

Design your flyers

Each mail should feature a single message, and that message should be clearly defined in the entire flyer. For instance, if you are searching for new sellers, then your message should introduce your services to distressed property owners. On the flyer, you need to avoid putting every detail about other properties that you are selling, or anything that can interfere with your message.

Call to Action (CTA)

Each marketing piece you develop should finish with a call to action. The CTA should summarize the message in your flyer and encourage your readers to take action. For example, the flyer describing who you are to prospective sellers can finish with a CTA that says:

Get in touch with me today by phone or email to learn more about how I can assist you in selling your home fast.

By the time the reader comes to read your CTA, they shall have all the information they need to make a decision. The CTA encourages readers to act on that decision instantly and take whichever action you want them to do.

Developing mailing lists

Building a list of prospective real estate sellers are going to require a lot of energy and time to update regularly. It is often a great idea to separate seller lists depending on the place where you got the information to simplify the process of updating lists regularly. You can build lists of possible sellers by:

Getting in touch with local banks to discuss getting lists of properties either in foreclosure or close to attaining a foreclosure. You will be shocked at the number of banks ready to offer this information.

Look online for any listings of vacant properties to see whether the owners are interested in selling the properties.

Reading published lists of bankruptcies in the local newspaper.

They are making use of lists in the newspaper titles "Recent Notice of Default" that will indicate the kind of property that owners want to sell because they are delaying on their mortgages.

Invest in real estate software that will personalize the searches online for homes with a specific amount of equity. Sometimes, people who have a lot of equity in their homes may want to sell homes quickly and gather their equity.

Visit your local city hall to look for lists of property owners who live out-of-state and who are interested in selling their local properties.

Get in touch with the local fire department to ask whether you can be given a list of properties recently destroyed by fire. You can still follow the local fire and police calls in the newspaper every day to get addresses of destroyed properties.

List brokers

The internet has a lot of companies that are ready to create custom real estate property lists depending on your criteria.

Creating an effective campaign

Your direct mail skills always evolve as you learn more about how the process work, and the process that doesn't work. For instance, try to apply a handwritten-looking font on one type of mailer and then a decent font on the other. Monitor the responses you receive and take advantage of the strategy that gets a lot of responses.

Your direct email piece will compete directly with other real estate wholesalers, which is the reason why you need to monitor each result for every mailer and learn from the good and bad responses. Maybe you discover that a handwritten-looking envelope integrated with a professional looking direct mail letter is the right mix to get results. Each moment you learn something from your previous direct mail campaigns, you must use that information to make the next one better.

The message

What type of message works best with each audience? You may realize that people who possess abandoned homes respond better to professional looking messages, while those nearing a foreclosure prefer an informal approach. You need to note down these observations and apply them to build messages that work well for every audience.

Costs

It is important that you are always on the lookout for methods to ensure your direct mailing costs stay low. Monitor your track costs and ensure that you compare your costs to your tenants. You can still reduce your costs by regularly updating your lists and searching bulk mail discounts.

If you purchase from list brokers, then it is important to monitor the results you get with the lists and avoid using brokers that will send you bad addresses. You may also want to ensure that your lists receive responses that generate revenue to avoid wasting money on the future lists.

MailMerge And Custom Mailings

MailMerge is a program that works directly with the Microsoft Excel application to assist in building custom envelopes and letters for each contact you have. With the MailMerge, you can create fields from Excel and complete in your letter and envelope templates using custom information. Below is how MailMerge operates:

Outsourcing

You can always outsource your direct mail campaigns to an experienced organization that is focused on these types of marketing tactics. With a great outsourcing company, you can free yourself and get more sellers to expand your inventory.

Direct mail is a great marketing tool for any type of real estate wholesaler. Once your lists are updated correctly, and you continue to run experiments until you discover the correct message for every audience, you will begin to find the resources you require to build your business.

Driving for dollars is one of the real estate wholesaler marketing strategies that require the discovery of properties that may not appear on any list compiled. There are numerous methods to apply the drive for dollars' strategy, and you will finally build your own method depending on your experience. Some wholesalers prefer to apply the driving for dollars' campaign over compiling lists from online research. However, successful wholesalers understand that they must use each available strategy to get properties to represent.

This section will show you on the process of assessing properties and adding them to your potential list. Driving for dollars is a strategy of looking for properties in your neighborhood while driving. It is as simple as getting into your car and, starting to scour properties near your neighborhood. While it appears simple, there is a lot of preparation that you need to do before you go hunting.

This strategy is still your opportunity to interact with the residents of your neighborhoods and introduce yourself. This is the point where you employ your negotiation skills and professional presentation skills. The friendlier and approachable you become, the more information you gain from residents concerning a distressed property. Driving for dollars will not only allow you to add properties to your inventory, but it will also assist you to increase your referral network.

How to get started with driving for dollars

As with any plan for marketing in real estate, the driving for the dollar isn't something that you should wake up and decide to do. It is critical that you spend time to compile a list and highlight neighborhoods that you want to drive through before you get into the field. You can decide to select your own method for determining the type of neighborhoods to visit. Here are some ideas for you:

The average age of homes. Possible equity in the homes

Crime percent rate. A lower crime percent makes it easier to sell properties to house flippers.

The challenge with driving for dollars without a strategy is that you don't have a hint of what type of properties you are looking for. Keep in mind that time is valuable, and you want to ensure that you optimize your return anytime you are marketing.

Things that you should have

As you prepare to go driving, you should look for the following things:

A camera

Your business cards to give to your neighborhood.

Flies that describe your business to provide your neighborhood people. Your lists

Tips for finding the best moments to drive for dollars

When you focus on a specific neighborhood for dollars, any property near that neighborhood is a good game. However, there are some clues that you must look for to show that a property is distressed, or the owners are going through certain problems that may result in a distressed property in the coming future.

Here are the best tips to use to locate possible properties while driving for dollars:

Properties that don't have an outdoor decoration for Christmas, or interior decorations seen via the windows. This may show a religious preference, but it can also be a great sign of a distressed property.

Properties that have developed newspapers on the porch that are cleaned once or twice a month. Properties with garbage collection in different places.

Properties featuring boarded up doors, or windows. Properties without lights on at night.

Properties attached with ordinance notice at the front doors.

Let dive into the process

It can take a few drives through a neighborhood before you make up your mind to drive for dollars. For example, it can take several weeks of constant driving through a neighborhood to select the properties that don't put their garbage out on collection day. However, once you gather all the information necessary, it is time to go driving through for dollars.

While you drive through the neighborhood, you will use your camera to take pictures of properties you think may be prospective inventory items. Look for clear pictures of the worst features of the properties so that you can create accurate notes when you return to your office. Make use of the pen and paper to take note of the addresses you snapped pictures, and make notes on the status of the properties and neighborhood in general.

What you will be looking for

You will be searching for a distressed property that has out-of-state owners or is owner-occupied. These describe properties which you can market your services to the owners and receive immediate feedback. An abandoned property owned by banks needs a completely different process for buying. You need to separate the bank owned properties and concentrate on the properties that you can contact.

You can look for owners of these properties via your county's Central Appraisal District (CAD). Your local CAD is easy to get by using Google. The CAD will show you who possesses the property, and it will further provide you with the contact information for out-of-state owners as well. You can use your smartphone to connect with the CAD while you are in the field to avoid wasting time to process bank-owned properties, or you can confirm the CAD when you reach to the office and separate the bank-owned properties from the rest.

Processing your information

The information you gather while driving for dollars can be inserted on a spreadsheet that is different from the rest of your information to ensure that marketing is simple. Once you get a property to add to your possible pool, you must record the way you found that property so that you can send the correct type of marketing piece to the property owner.

When you go back to your office, you will take all the addresses you have gathered and begin to create an owner contact list depending on your findings. Make sure you attach your photos to each list entry to notify yourself of why you placed that property on your list in the first place.

Of course, abandoned properties are clear as to why they are distressed, but the owner-occupied properties you come across is going to be a bit difficult to classify. You aim to generate a thousand dollars from properties that aren't on any pre-foreclosure list you have created. Driving for dollars prevents these properties from being picked by others, but you may have to apply a customized marketing piece to speak to homeowners who currently occupy distressed homes effectively.

While you drive for dollars, you may be asked by the residents who are a bit curious to know why you are doing it. These are people whom you can speak to about relaying your information on other distressed properties in the area, or they may own a distressed property of their own. Driving for dollars involves the way you will reach out to communities where you work and build good relationships with the local people.

Some advice on the best approach

If you begin knocking on the doors of distressed property owners, then you may experience solicitation challenges. Besides, your purpose of looking for dollars is to find properties to add to your list. Therefore, knocking on the doors can slow down your efforts rather than optimize your results.

When a distressed property is owned by a landlord and occupied by tenants, then you may not want to attempt to leave any information with the tenants. Your target should be on the property owners and not anyone else. You may even get into trouble for leaving a real estate wholesaling with a tenant who has no idea that their property is distressed.

The correct approach to optimize the driving for dollars' campaign is to develop a plan and realize exactly what you are searching for when you are in the field. Driving for dollars involves finding properties that do not appear on any of your lists, and that it will assist you to be a step ahead of the competition.

When you decide that wholesaling is the thing that you want to do in your career, you must instantly drive yourself into what you do if you want to realize success. The more people you speak to, and the more familiar you become with the location you are working in, the information you will have to expand your business. Once you have a detailed knowledge of your territory and the way things operate within that territory, then you will be boosting yourself on the competition.

Few activities in marketing assist you to discover everything you want to know concerning the geographic location you are working in such as door knocking. When you take advantage of door knocking to make yourself known to the people in the area where you work, you tend to allow yourself to build a strong bond with the community that can result in a never-ending source of property referrals. There is a lot to door knocking than just moving from one property to the next and introducing yourself. Once you discover how to optimize the door knocking strategy, you will start to see why many successful wholesalers use it often.

Door knocking. What is it?

As the name goes, you move from door to door and introduce yourself to property owners in a specific neighborhood. You are directed by a list of potential sellers created from your research. You can take the door knocking one street at a time, or you can decide to be ambitious and attempt to cover the whole neighborhood at once. For you to become effective, it is important to knock on a door twice a year to confirm that your name and business remain as fresh as possible in the minds of people.

Why should you go back to door knocking?

Many people who live in neighborhoods dislike seeing abandoned properties reduce the property values and result in criminals living in the area. Door knocking is an excellent method to discover the type of properties in an abandoned area.

Searching for distressed properties that don't appear like distressed

Sometimes it is hard to tell a book by its cover, and each wholesaler in the area may be walking by a distressed house and not even realize. You may knock on the door of the beautiful looking property and learn that the owner is three months behind paying their mortgage and wants to sell it quickly. You will know this because you came across an address while researching on pre-foreclosures with different banks.

Create a referral network

Many wholesalers use door knocking with the main purpose of building a large referral network with the local people. For instance, you can develop a flyer that promises to pay each resident with $100 for each property they direct your way that you finally get a buyer. It will cost you zero to set up a massive referral network with residents, but it can generate a stream of great property referrals. Regardless of the type of list your prospective generates, they can all become an important part of your network that generates more leads to your business.

Develop a reputation as that kind of person who can assist homeowners

Building a good reputation among distressed property owners in a place where you want to sell properties is highly going to support your business. As you go knocking doors of property owners and explain to people the way you can assist distressed homeowners, you will learn that people in these neighborhoods go beyond their abilities to suggest to you homeowners who may need your services.

Develop a system

Door knocking is something that you will want to make it a regular part of your business marketing strategy. You will conduct a lot of marketing for your wholesaling business, but few marketing techniques provide you with benefits than door knocking. When you build a list of prospective, then purpose to get into the neighborhoods and see those properties. Your door knocking procedures should be directed by the lists you build from the many hours of research. Time is important in real estate wholesaling, and the earlier you introduce yourself to distressed property owners, the earlier you can make money by assisting them in selling their properties.

The odds that you will end a deal to represent a property while knocking on the door depends on the quality of your list. However, the more doors you knock, the larger your referral network grows, and the more goodwill you will develop all of the homeowners in your local area. It may take time for the door knocking to pay off, but when it does pay, it can be the most successful forms of marketing you will ever do.

Bandit signs/ yard signs

Also known as yard signs, these are signs where you post near towns in places that can be easily seen. You can post them in the property yards you are currently listing, real estate attorneys, title insurance companies, and any other form of business that handles real estate transactions. The most critical thing is to ensure that you put your yard signs in places where many people will see them. Yard signs are affordable and easy to install.

Bandit signs are posted on telephone poles and any place that they can be seen by traffic. Typically, you want to post them at intersections and junctions where traffic stops so that people can read the signs. There are different ways of making bandit signs, and it is vital that you research well to know the types of signs that are effective in specific areas of your area.

Placing signs

There are still other great places where you can place the signs. The walls outside popular sports stadiums and light poles are excellent areas to put your signs because people tend to spend most of their time waiting in line, or preparing for the game. The same is true for popular nightclubs around your city.

If you get permission to post signs in parking ramps, then you will have a captive audience daily that will be reading your signs. Public parks can as well be great places for signs because many people visit the park and they have enough time to read a sign that draws their attention. In places where you are sure people will gather, you should make an effort to get your signs into visible places.

The advantage of the yard and bandit signs

Both yard and bandit signs are cheap and easy to acquire. There are different vendors online that offer excellent work for a low price. They capture the attention, and you will have a good percentage of people who will read the signs if you place them in the correct places.

Great signs will push your brand and get people to identify your company name on sight. Signs also draw the attention of buyers, investors, and sellers to help you develop your database of contacts.

The drawbacks of the yard and bandit signs

Some communities have banned these signs, which could mean more trouble if you use them. Your yard signs posted on public property could result in police and asked to pay fines. Bandit signs removed from telephone lines could lead to serious legal effects for you that will worsen in case you are marked as a repeat offender.

Some wholesalers look at fines as the cost of doing business because their yard and bandit signs generate a continuous stream of a lucrative business. However, it might reach the point where you are handling more than a few fines because of the constant signs.

What you should know before getting into real estate property wholesaling

It takes the right individual to be in the right place for success. As a result, before you can get into real estate wholesaling, take time to decide whether wholesaling will work for you in the real estate sector. Now, this is not a move to sweet talk you out of it, but a word of encouragement to you that you assess the situation first and decide whether you want to do it or not. For you to wholesale real estate properties, you need to have the correct real estate knowledge and education. You also need to have the right connections and the correct negotiation skills. These are important factors in real estate wholesaling.

Additionally, you need to consider the pros and cons of real estate wholesaling. Although wholesaling is the best solution to the question, "How to make money in real estate?", the challenge is that it's not guaranteed. What this really means is that if you fail to get a property buyer, you would have wasted a lot of time. This is the same reason why you must have connections when using these investment strategies. Networks simplify the process of getting clients, your case; they are called buyers.

One of the main things of wholesaling investment properties is learning the housing market. Real estate wholesaling can be one of the quickest means to learn more about the real estate market. As a result, diving into it will provide you with a great experience improvement.

Lastly, real estate wholesaling is a great thing as long as you are aware of what you are getting into. But this doesn't mean that you cannot involve other profitable investment methods. It only means that you need to take into account the shortcomings and find a way forward.

CHAPTER 5

Real Estate Investment Deals

When it comes to investment properties, the most commonly asked question is where a person can get funding for the next deal.

If you are thinking of purchasing a house for investment, but you don't have sufficient money in your bank account, don't worry. Fortunately, there are many financing opportunities than you know. Picking the right choice for your investment strategy and specific instance save you a huge amount of money.

In this section, you will learn about the various loans available for financing your next real estate investment.

1. Conventional loans

This is one of the most common types of mortgage. In a conventional loan, you pay a certain amount of money before the bank provides you with the remaining money. Although a lot of banks let borrowers pay as little as 5% of the buying price, investors have no option but put down more than that. As such, many investors pay a down payment of 20%, so that the loan is not considered as part of the private mortgage insurance. (PMI).

Advantages

Easy to understand

The most common type of financing, so it is easy to shop around for the best terms and rates. Conventional loans are one of the lowest interest rates for any loan options.

Disadvantages

Conventional loans have a limit.

You require to have a credit score of more than 640 to qualify.

It is a bit difficult to qualify if you purchase properties using LLC instead of putting them in your name.

2. Veteran Affairs (VA) loan

Getting a VA loan is a great achievement of working in the military. This loan provides no-down-payment loans to veterans, chosen military spouses, and service members. Same to FHA loan, you will have to stay in the home for a minimum of one year. One good thing with this type of loan is that you can purchase as many houses as you would like as long as you don't surpass the set amount, and you stay in each one for a minimum of one year. The limiting aspect isn't the number of houses; it is the amount you are awarded.

Advantages

PMI not needed for VA loans. It has the lowest interest rate.

No down payment. Very low closing costs. With the VA loans, the seller will have to pay for some of the closings costs the buyer would always pay.

A high ratio of debt-to-income allowed.

You can correctly develop a portfolio of rental properties without any down payment by living in every house for a year, or renting out each and moving on.

Disadvantages

Not available to everyone.

You will need to live in the property for at least one year. A lot of paperwork at the time of settlement.

There is a specific VA funding charge that is included in your loan that the VA asks to ensure the program continues to run.

3. 203(k) loan

The 203(k) loan resembles the FHA loan because it is centered a lot toward homeowners than investors. This is an owner-occupied, 3.5% down payment loan that lets you lump the rehab costs into the mortgage.

Advantages

You can support the entire project with one lender.

You can expand the choices to include distressed and foreclosed homes.

You can request a better deal on a property that deserves rehab, which means you can gain immediate equity.

If you do the rehab work yourself, you can move on to discuss the costs below the retail process.

No need to look for additional money for rehab costs, and when you are done, the home will possibly be worth more than the loan amount.

Disadvantages

Contractors have to be voted and approved by your lender.

Only accessible to owner-occupants- you must live at the property as your main residence. In general, the amount of paperwork is more during and after settlement.

4. Private money

This one refers to finances from individual investors. There are no institutions involved here. In this method, you can ask for support from family, co-workers, or a few close friends you have interacted with at your local real estate investing groups. In general, private money will be costlier than a traditional mortgage. However, the terms set are more flexible. Additionally, the requirements to qualify for this type of funding is friendly.

Pros

Cons

Minimum qualifications are demanded. Has a simple and flexible structure.

Has a higher interest rate than other loans.

You may need to look for an attorney to create a financial contract. The terms are shorter (3-5) years.

In case things don't go well, it may destroy the relationship between you and the lender.

5. Hard money

This resembles private money; the only difference is that the money doesn't come from an individual but a hard- money lender. For this type of loan, the lender uses a hard asset to protect the loan. Hard money is a form of short- term loan used by borrowers to purchase fix up and flip. In general, you can get hard money to account for 70-80% of the property bought before rehab. Just like private money, hard-money lenders cut a huge interest and include other charges such as origination fees.

Pros

Cons

It is easy to get because the loan is protected by property. Has a simple and flexible loan structure.

Lenders of hard money know the special needs of real estate investors and provide quick loan funding and approval.

The rate of interest is higher than other loans.

It can be quite expensive if a person is thought to be risky.

There are many methods to employ to finance your real estate investment deals. Understanding everything about each method is crucial. It is important that you consider all the available options rather than jump into traditional methods of financing. Find time to discuss your methods and choices with a professional loan officer who has interacted with investors and develop the best financing plan for your situations, knowing that those situations change over time.

The world has people who are looking for great places to invest their money. Therefore, if you have a good record of generating profit with your real estate investment, then getting a financing option will not be a big problem for you. You may need to become a bit creative.

Find the best deals and the investing strategies

People continue to join real estate to generate wealth, and the more people want to purchase real estate properties, the harder it becomes to find deals. It is that simple as supply and demand in business.

As a result, the method that investors employed to find deals in the past is quickly changing. Unlike a few years ago where it was possible to get a deal using MLS, today is almost impossible. But instead, smart investors are redefining their methods of finding deals. At the end of the day, if you want something that no one else can get, it is a must that you do something that no one else will do to earn.

So, are you ready to learn what to do what everyone is not doing? If yes, here are a few methods that you can apply to strike a great deal.

Let's start!

1. Try to purchase foreclosed properties from a bank.

When a person fails to pay his or her mortgage for a certain period, the lender will decide to repossess the property and chase away the occupants. Once the house is empty, the lender goes on to list the house for sale on the market, by using a local real estate channel.

While the foreclosure is a sad thing, these homes can be one of the best deals you can come across in real estate. Banks will always want to remain in the business of lending money, and not maintaining homes or houses, so they are always quick to provide massive discounts just to remove the deal from their records. But though these are one of the best deals ever, you can only strike a great deal on foreclosed properties, if you know the methods of purchasing foreclosures.

Since the foreclosure process requires different years; these properties require serious updating and repair. In this case, more discounts may be generated to compensate the buyers.

2. Make sure you are the first or the last.

In real estate business, the early bird always catches the worm. Sometimes, it is not the highest offer for a property that is accepted; it's but the first. As a result, if you are searching for a great deal, you must be quick to snatch it. Look for pre-approval from a bank so that you can jump at any property anytime, and let your real estate agent set you up to receive automatic email alerts reminding you of new property that comes to the market.

Next, don't wait for anything but check it out immediately, and send an offer the same day if you can.

Alternatively, you can also find the best deals by looking at properties that have been in the market for a long time. The owners of these properties are usually ready to sell for a discount because they are tired of holding on to the same property. In most cases, they may have been making two mortgage payments and will accept any offer.

3. Look for absent property owners privately.

In a competitive real estate, great deals can be very difficult to find because of the huge number of people hunting for a house. In some places, a single home for sale may receive more than a dozen offers in the first few days.

As a result, the best trick real estate investors employ today to get in touch with contact owners and ask them to sell. At any moment, a great percentage of the population will listen to this option, so why should you not reach out to them before they list it with a real estate agent?

The best people to focus on is absentee owners; these are individuals who own a given property but don't live there. They could be landlord or owners who have inherited their houses and are not sure what to do with them. You can get these deals in different ways, such as:

Purchasing public record list.

Searching for houses that appear vacant.

Making a call to mom-and-pop landlords who have listed properties “for rent” on the Craigslist. Tell them that you are not interested in renting the property, but you would like to speak with them about purchasing.

4. Eviction records

Evictions aren’t a good thing. It is messy, time-intensive, and costly. During the time of eviction, many landlords start to ask questions about why they are involved in this game.

This is the reason why focusing on landlords who are in the process of an eviction can be so good. They are experiencing a problem, and there is a good chance they will be happy to get out of the property quickly.

Well, how can you target these landlords?

Evictions are an aspect of public record in many counties of America. This means that you can visit your local county administration office and request to see a list of the current evictions happening. Various counties and states conduct evictions in different ways, but if you ask it shouldn’t be difficult to find.

5. Direct mail

Lastly, you must recognize that finding the best deals is possibly a 'numbers game.' So if you have a list of people who can be your potential sellers, you can decide to send them letters, having the belief that a small percentage may call you to discuss, and a few of those may end up selling you their properties.

Although this may look cheap on the surface, direct email marketers know that the proof lies in the percentages. Lastly, if you remain passionate about your goal to find sellers, then you will possibly find many. One thing that you must know is that people are always ready to help you accomplish your goals, you need to let the world know what you want, and the rest will help you get it.

How to analyze deals and make offers?

As a real estate investor, you can either build or destroy your investment when you pay a lot for a property; you may end up losing all your shorts. Find a great deal on a home, and it may make a big difference.

Some programs exist that promise you to get deals from the comfort of your home. As long as you have a stable internet connection, a computer, and a telephone you are in business. But remember when the deal is so good, think twice. The truth is that there is a lot that is done apart from playing around with numbers.

While feelings can dictate whether you will buy a property or not, there is a lot more than just your feelings. Typically, you want a real estate deal that will fulfill your goals. To realize that, you must know how to analyze and value the property, including predicting whether it's going to generate money.

Your responsibility as you assess various properties is to ignore the list of prices, or what the sellers might want and concentrate on what is important to you.

Don't be scared about the property assessment of the city or whether the sellers paid for it. Those numbers aren't that important. You might use them while negotiating if it comes to that point, but for the sake of analyzing the property, they are not necessary.

As you assess the property, pay attention to the following things:

What is the place zoned out for? What else can you add there? Can you create an office space or more units?

Are there any regulations or rules set on the use of the property? What are the forms of transport near the property?

What status is the property in?

Are there any problems caused by the environment near the property? This can be bed bugs, earthquakes, termites, mold and many more.

Who are the occupants? Owners of the property or tenants?

What else is in the area that is attractive for someone living there? Does it have parks?

What is your gut telling you when you set eyes on the property? How is the experience when you are in the property?

Some of the things mentioned here you can check using google maps and gather other information from the internet. However, many of these questions require that you show up physically in the property to answer them accurately.

Next, to determine the values, you will require to run the same analysis on other properties that are on the market, including the ones that have been sold recently in the area. You will also need to look for time to calculate the rent rate you can earn for the property.

In case you find two properties with the same size and location, but one is more expensive than the other, it is your task to find out why. Remember, the cheaper property could be in a worse location. Or it could be in a noisy street, or close to a garbage dump where it receives less sunlight. These are just a few of the many things that you will have to figure out.

Things you need to analyze a real estate deal and compute the cash flow

You will require to collect most of the following information to determine the cash flow:

Property taxes. Property maintenance Recycling/garbage fee Rent

Electricity Heat

Aside from this, you will need to develop a rough idea of how much you will require to pay as a down payment. Most of the items listed above can be estimated until you receive an accepted offer on the property, at which point you will have an easy route to the real numbers. But the more actual numbers you get from the seller and your different sources, the more accurate your cash flow prediction will be.

Ways to determine whether a property is a great real estate deal

Every property buyer wants a great deal while buying a real estate. Although the price is important, finding a property that can be destroyed with the least effort and time cannot be that easy. Anyone who buys a house with the purpose to fix it up to understands that there could be hidden challenges that arise without warning and aren't easy to identify, even if you have the best home assessment. The ability to tell whether a house is worth its investment requires a keen eye. Here are tips that you can use to tell whether a property can be a great deal.

1. Determine zoning problems and liens

In general, one way that you can know is when a property has a complication that may result in automatic "no" for most investors. Zoning problems and liens on a little non-institutional grade property are the best spots.

2. Stick to the 1% rule

There are different methods to review an investment return when purchasing an income property. As a rule of thumb, clients are advised to use the 1% rule that demands the income property should rent for around 1% of the buying price to generate positive cash flow.

3. Review the CAP Rate

Cap rate is one great signal, although there are some sensible reasons for a few sellers to become motivated than others. Also, the price per square foot or the price per door vs. neighborhood comps as good metrics if used well.

4. Look at the roofline

This can help you to see if the house appears sturdy, simple, elegant, vulnerable, or weak.

5. Develop a sense of condition and presentation

The status of the property plus how it has been presented will determine whether the property can be bought at a discount. So in case, the property doesn't have an online photo, then it probably has a zero-curb appeal. It also implies that a substantial discount can be asked on the buying price and the listing agent doesn't have a lot of work to do, and may just after a quick sale.

CHAPTER 6

Secrets of successful real estate investors

Since 2008, real estate investment has made most American accumulate lots of money. Based on a report by Morgan Stanley, around 77% of millionaire's have an investment in real estate. Do you want to join this group of rich men and women? Are you wondering what their secret could be? Fortunately, generating money with real estate is not a miracle

1. Make the necessary plan first

Starting real estate without a plan isn't the right thing to do. Before you dive in, define specific goals and objectives.

First, develop your plan. Next, you look for a house to suit that plan. Select your investment model, and then start to look for homes to match that. Don't look for a strategy once you find the property.

2. Become serious with agreements

Remember that contracts are a critical plus the agreement of buying and selling a property for a home. Contracts have a clear request including the consequence, time, and terms. You need to make sure that you completely understand all the requirements before you sign.

3. Remove your calculator

According to a real estate expert Scott McGillivray, numbers are vital in this business. Once you invest in a property, you must learn to enjoy performing different calculations. Don't be too focused on the house.

4. Buyer Beware

Real estate agents possess their own code. So you must be smart and learn to read between the line when scanning through listings.

5. Treat your real estate investment like a business

To achieve the success, you must work at it. You must become an active landlord, and monitor everything that is happening with your rental properties. Stay ahead of maintenance and repairs. Maintain great records. Don't look for shortcuts but follow the rules. If you can treat your real estate business with the required attention, you are likely to make the right decisions based on facts and numbers, instead of emotions.

6. Prepare for a long-term commitment

Don't be deceived by the get-rich schemes. Real estate is a long-term investment despite its state of illiquidity. It requires hard work, commitment and time. You will not get rich overnight, but when you do it right, real estate generates a good profit on investment.

7. Continue learning

The people who have made it in real estate know that there is always something to learn. As a result, many of them spend countless hours reading books, listings, or anything that they can get their hands on. Once they possess properties, they are faced with new types of challenges. Fortunately, many of them have experienced those challenges, and by reading useful real estate material, one can know how to handle a given problem. However, you can never find an answer to a problem if you stop researching and reading helpful material. Therefore, make sure that you never stop learning.

8. Now get out from your comfort zone

You will never make money in real estate if you decide to sit in one place every day. You must get out and start to research. You must be willing to meet your fellow investors and landlords. Walk through properties. Send different offers, even low ones. A real estate kingdom isn't built in a single day. It can take months to find the correct property at the right place. However, you will never find it if you don't research homes and scan through possible investments. So jump in!

9. Ask for help

Learning the tricks of succeeding in real estate is quite difficult for someone who wants to do things on their own. The best real estate investors attribute a fraction of their success to others. These can be lawyers, mentors, or any supportive friend. Instead of risking your time and money to solve a complex problem, you can also employ the expertise of other people.

10. Develop a network

A network is key in supporting and creating opportunities for both experienced and new real estate investors. This group should consist of a mentor, members of a non-profit organization, business partners and clients. Since most of the real estate investing depend on experimental learning, smart real estate investors know they need to build a network.

CONCLUSION

Up until this point we have looked at many different topics in real estate investment. As such, we believe that you know how to find the best investment properties in real estate, you have understood the concept of house flipping, property wholesaling, how to identify the best real estate investment deals and many more.

So.... what next?

The next step is to take a realistic review of yourself. Ask yourself the following questions:

1. Why do I want to invest in real estate? Are you getting into real estate just because you got laid off or you want to protect your retirement plan? How you respond to this question will set the tone for how you do everything else.

2. What are your skills, knowledge, and abilities in real estate?

3. What is your financial strength? This is important because if you don't have the funds or access to funds, your choices will be less.

4. How much time can you commit to real estate investing? If you are working on a full-time job and have a family. You will have to be fair to yourself. Don't deceive yourself that you are going to work an extra 30 hours a week on real estate. You will only discourage yourself.

5. Do you have a plan, even a general plan that describes where you want to be in your real estate business say in a year, three years, etc.? This is also necessary because as you gain more experience more opportunities emerge.

6. What are some of the non-financial resources available?

While there are other questions that you need to ask yourself, the success of your real estate business will revolve around the time and response to the above questions. Spending time to "get it right" at the start will prevent many challenges that may arise down the road.

YouTube Marketing

Table of Contents

Introduction:

Why Use YouTube for Marketing?

In 2017, digital marketing has taken on completely new forms. New methods of digital marketing are expanding as the industry becomes increasingly diversified across different platforms. This is both positive and negative news for online marketers. Depending on how well they can adapt and react to these changes, this can either be a hurdle or a great new opportunity for growth. It's going to be important, now, to utilize more than one media channel to both grow your brand and spread your content.

The Changing Face of Marketing:

Marketing was once easy, simple to attract viewers and create your own website, but now, due to the saturation of the market, the Internet is very competitive out there for those who wish to earn online. Drawing in an audience is no longer as easy as before since there are so many other sites competing to get audience attention. The following chapters will discuss some of the many ways you can stay relevant with your brand, or even create one from scratch, using YouTube. The final chapter will explore what to do beyond basic YouTube marketing. But first...

Why Use YouTube for Marketing?

Creating ads and content that attracts people means something different than it did before. Interactive content and virtual reality are of the risk now, and according to experts, YouTube views are going to become more important than ever.

- **To Create an Authority-based Image:** As mentioned, marketing is changing now, and YouTube has a lot to do with that. It's an essential tool for marketing no matter which company you're involved with or plan to become involved with. Uploading and importing videos is easier than ever, making it nearly effortless to add to your existing business plan. For companies, marketing using online videos offers a new opportunity that wasn't there before. Used the right way, and video marketing can help establish your company as being an authoritative voice on a matter.

- **A Huge Platform:** Another reason to take advantage of YouTube marketing is for the simple reason that it's the second largest online search engine that exists, offering your company a large platform for gaining audience members. The average customer is no longer satisfied with static marketing or physical ads and instead want engaging, aesthetic interactive content. Uploading video material gives users your ideas and business views, providing the aura of authority and expertise on the topic.

When you share video content with strategies and tips, you can attract attention to your customers while providing them with value, building up your image as a respectable source. This is what keeps clients coming back time and time again, helping your brand grow.

- **Popularity:** YouTube didn't take long at all to become established as a hugely popular website, and this doesn't appear to be changing. They get over a billion unique audience members each and every month and endless hours of video content is watched each minute by these people. But most people just use the site to watch video content. They watch what they want to watch, maybe leave a comment and subscribe, and then watch something else.

Unfortunately, a lot of people who view the video content of others are not piloting the show, but are acting as mere passengers. Deciding to make your own channel on YouTube puts you into the driver's seat, making your content widely available for the millions of viewers on the site every day.

More Benefits to YouTube Marketing:

Still not convinced? Let's go over some more of the benefits to using YouTube for marketing.

1. SEO Advantages:

When you make a channel on YouTube, your search engine results are moving up already. You can then choose to use your YouTube channel and videos to bring more users to your blog, which also helps with your search engine results. In addition, videos do better than blog posts when it comes to search engines. Google offers a distinct benefit for YouTube on its search results because Google owns this website. A huge amount of the revenue earned by Google is actually on YouTube.

2. More Chances to be Discovered.

One very interesting piece of information about social media and shopping pages is that these websites are actually also search engines. YouTube is considered a search engine too, just as Google is. The search engine on Google lets you discover anything you want, but the search engine on YouTube will only seek out video content that is already on the site. YouTube isn't as big as Google is, of course, but it still gets a huge amount of unique visitors each month, as mentioned before. These users will be coming back over and over again and usually stay on YouTube for more than 10 minutes each session. This means that those who like what you make will come back to watch more of your content.

3. Your Content can Earn you More.

It's no secret that YouTube is great for sharing your message and promoting your blog, but did you know that YouTube itself is also profitable? People can actually earn millions from using Google AdSense with their existing video content. In fact, videos have made more than $100k, even those that are short (under two minutes in length). Envision it taking only a couple minutes to make a video, then earning that much from it! This is possible on YouTube, and it's an opportunity you shouldn't ignore.

True, the odds that you will hit it that big aren't very good, but you can still increase your subscribers and get up to thousands of views a day as time goes on. You can then expect to earn hundreds with YouTube. In addition, if your channel becomes very popular, you can start earning thousands each day.

There are plenty of books on this subject on the market, thanks again for choosing this one! Every effort was made to ensure it is full of as much useful information as possible. Please enjoy!

Chapter 1:

Setting up a YouTube Brand

Nothing brings more satisfaction than getting to a huge milestone when it comes to your YouTube channel and brand. The first milestone you can celebrate is the initial 1,000 subscribers. Making it to this many subscribers seems impossible to those who are new to the idea, but it's easier than you think!

Tips for Getting 1,000 Subscribers:

Throughout this book, we are going to give you tips on getting more and more subscribers until eventually, you can make it to 100,000 and beyond. As we will mention throughout the book, YouTube works best in conjunction with other websites and social networks and can be used as a catalyst to improve your business and audience. Let's cover some basic rules for enjoying a successful journey with YouTube.

Be Consistent:

To be successful with YouTube, you must post content that is valuable and do it on a consistent basis. This is actually quite challenging. Just looking around the website will lead you to think that every topic has already been made and even though that isn't true, you can take a topic that's already popular and put your own unique spin on it. For instance, a lot of techs "unboxing" videos exist, but you could make a "re-boxing" channel where you discuss different tech components as you place them in their box. This is just an idea, but feel free to be creative and come up with something on your own.

Give your Videos Smart Names:

Another challenging aspect of YouTube content creation is coming up with a good title for your videos. You may have an idea already, but it could be too long or complicated. Stick with the rule of keeping it as basic as you can, and YouTube can auto-complete the name. It doesn't matter if your video has a similar name to an existing video, but it does have to apply and make sense. If you are having a hard time coming up with quality names, there is a lot of extra information on the web about naming your videos successfully. Don't forget to do your research!

Make the Design of your Channel Appealing:

A lot of visitors are gathering a first impression of your brand and idea based on the design of your channel. This is how audience members can interact with you and learn what your channel stands for. Make an appealing header to showcase your company or brand. If you aren't very skilled with graphic design, font, or color selection, there are professionals online who are willing to help for a reasonable fee. In addition, you could ask a tech-savvy friend in your life to help you create an engaging channel style.

Try out Different Shooting Locations:

You can make your channel instantly more interesting by shooting videos in different areas. This could be challenging if you only have access to one area, but even changing up the background or going to a local coffee shop to record every once in a while can help keep your videos interesting to your audience members. This will keep them guessing and interested to return to see what you will do next.

Be Lighthearted:

It's no fun to watch someone that's too serious all the time, so try to poke fun at yourself and laugh on your channel every once in a while. Making mistakes openly allows you to appear more human to your audience, showing a different side than most of the other basic talking head content videos out there. Try to make it fresh, exciting, and spontaneous, so your viewers are surprised when they come to your channel. But in addition to this, always be yourself.

If you are the humorous type, make sure you show that in your videos. If you are serious, be yourself. What people will respond to and appreciate the most is someone genuine and relatable. You may not be liked by everyone, but you will be appreciated by the ones who matter.

Utilize the Custom Thumbnail Option:

You can increase your views and subscriptions on YouTube with this simple change. Just use a font that is popular on different photos online to get attention, then you can adjust the photo in Photoshop. You can make the title of the picture thumbnail something other than the video title so viewers can instantly tell what they are about to see.

Make Use of Annotations:

Have you ever been watching a video and see those little pop ups in the middle? Using these can be really helpful for making your content more effective. For each video, add an annotation to make subscribing to your channel easier for viewers. Sure, this does take a little extra effort, but as soon as you watch your rate of subscriptions increase, you'll want annotations in all of your videos.

Don't be Afraid to Ask:

This is a simple but often overlooked tip. You cannot get what you don't ask for! When your videos end, make sure you ask them to both subscribe and "like" your video and channel. This is a good time to also tell what audience members can expect from your channel. For instance, if you focus on home improvement project tips, you can tell users to subscribe to get more tips on the subject.

Be True to Yourself:

We already discussed this a bit above, but it's worth going into again. Always be yourself on your videos and channel! You can only be yourself and nothing else, even when you try. Some find being in front of the camera hard initially because you want to compare yourself to those who are skilled at being in front of the camera. Get over this by realizing that fakeness doesn't get you anywhere. Instead, allow your true personality to come through, and you will draw people towards you who resonate with who you are.

Make a Quality Trailer for Your Channel:

YouTube now gives video makers the chance to design their channel, including a trailer to cover what the channel is about. Most people only go see movies when they have already seen the trailer and can know what to expect. Your trailer should be no longer than a minute and a half, providing some scenes from the content you have on your channel along with reasons to subscribe. People will keep coming back if you put real effort into what you make.

<u>The Third Most Popular Site Online:</u>

YouTube is definitely number one in terms of video creation social networking, but it's also the third most visited site online. Yet not many people are taking full advantage of the social networking abilities it brings. Most users on YouTube don't even use the platform to create a brand, build their own presence, or make money. A lot of users haven't even put one video onto YouTube. If you're completely new to this idea, it's time to think about YouTube in a more serious way. Here are some reasons why:

- **Cross Promotion:** It's possible to cross promote using YouTube, using it to get viewers to your other websites or blogs. When your videos end, make sure you tell audience members that they can find you on your blog. Don't forget to remind them to subscribe, as well. YouTube is okay on its own, but where it's truly useful is as a supplement to existing blogs or websites. For this to work, you must engage in cross promotion on a regular basis for your channel.

- **A Full-Time Income can Happen:** Yes, it's possible, some have made full-time incomes from YouTube alone, especially through the AdSense program Google offers. When you first start out, however, make sure you are working on multiple income streams. AdSense really doesn't offer much money in comparison to the other strategies we are going to cover, but you still shouldn't ignore it.

- **A Chance to Grow your Business:** If you have videos on YouTube, people are likelier to watch your content. The more content you have, the longer they will watch it, and the longer they watch it, the higher the odds that they will end up subscribing to your content and finding your blog or other websites. Remember, the more, the better, but quality also matters!

The Importance of Optimized Titles:

Standing out from the crowd is the only way to have success on YouTube and one good way to accomplish this is by naming your videos something unique and offbeat. This will help people come to your channel due to curiosity. Having unique, quirky titles definitely plays a role in building up your views. However, in order to get as many views as you can, you have to know some SEO basics in terms of YouTube marketing. Here are some tips for that:

- **Title Keywords:** This was once a lot more effective for SEO than it is now, but it does still have an impact on your content. Crawlers on Google can't watch your videos the way they can read through text posts, so if you place your keywords into your video title, the bots on Google will be aware of the topic.

- **Utilize AdWords on Google:** In order to find out what search items are popular right now, utilize Google AdWords. Attempt to go for videos that have both low competition and high volume searches.

- **Have a Descriptive Title:** Although offbeat titles are a positive thing, you should also be giving your audience an idea of what your content is going to cover. Be unique but make sure that what your title says is relevant and makes sense in terms of what your video is about. This may take some practice to get good at, but you will if you keep at it.

- **Go for Shorter Titles for your Videos:** Keep in mind that Google shortens your video title down and puts "YouTube" before it, which takes up 10 more characters. Try to make your titles either 50 characters or shorter to maximize this.

- **Omit "Video" from the Video name:** There is no reason to include the word "video" when you are naming your video. This just eats up character space and doesn't help you in your YouTube search ratings. However, doing this might have a small impact on typical search results.

- **Customize your Channel:** When you are attempting to build trust with audience members using YouTube, you must use the options for customization on YouTube. Make it unique and fresh.

- **Be Professional:** Even though you are likely shooting your videos from your room, a professional appearance does matter in terms of gaining trust and respect from audience members. If your blog already has a following, try to use the same elements of branding on YouTube so others can recognize you across different websites and platforms.

Make a Bio: Make sure you use the channel bio option YouTube offers to make your channel fully customized. Your bio information should be to the point and short. Add a link to your website, store page, or blog in video descriptions.

- **Placing Subscribe Buttons on your Website:** As mentioned, you should definitely include a link to your blog or website on your YouTube videos, but don't forget to add subscribe buttons on your blog to your YouTube channel, as well.

- **Keep your Videos less than Five Minutes Long:** YouTube has no shortage of in-depth, detailed videos and content, but the videos that convert the most subscribers are shorter than five minutes long. In 2014, it was found that most videos on YouTube are about 4.4 minutes long, so for those of you just starting out, this is an ideal number to shoot for. This will help you build up a loyal following.

  As soon as you already have a following on your channel, you can play around with different lengths to see how people react, but at first, keep it entertaining, informative, simple, and short. It might be hard, but it's a worthy challenge and increases your likelihood of success with YouTube.

Having quality, custom-made art for your channel will go a long way in helping you get established with your brand online. YouTube has a service for channel art if you aren't skilled in graphic design.

Make sure you use a custom-made background head image with similar elements of design from your other website or blog.

Using the Best Tools with YouTube:

Plenty of useful tools exists to use with YouTube, including video creation tools, video promotion tools, and more. Making use of these will help you grow your subscribers in an organic way, and organic views mean more subscribers, over time. Here are some video marketing tools you can use to get the results you're looking for.

- **Bulk Suggest Tool:** This free tool was created by the Internet Marketing Ninjas and is an easy way to find out relevant keyword research data for your content. It will look through YouTube and Google's "auto complete" databases, expanding the terms you entered based on popular search terms. This allows you to compare search terms in Google fast with YouTube terms, better understanding the searching goals of your target subscribers and audience members.

  WordPress Keyword Plugin: In addition, there's a plugin for WordPress that you can use to look at keyword ideas using Google auto complete search terms. This is in your dashboard under the post editing options. Another benefit to this plugin is that it can give you ideas for what to create articles and videos about based on what is popular.

Do Research on Competitors:

Finding out more about your competitors will help you with your campaign for content marketing. Although this shouldn't get in the way of your creative ideas, analyzing your competitors will help you find out what works, along with tactics to help your viewers feel more interested and engaged in your channel. The best tool for this is the YouTube Analysis feature on BirdSong Analytics. This tool allows you to pay as you go. It only requires a channel name to use, and this handy tool will give you lots of useful reports and stats, such as:

- Your competitor's channel's best upload time (in terms of getting likes).
- The ideal day to upload for getting likes, according to your competitor.
- When you should upload to receive audience comments, according to the competition.
- The best day to upload videos in order to get comments, according to your competition's channel.
- The way the length of your videos can impact viewing figures.
- The way the length of the videos can impact viewer engagement.

- Commonly used terms in video captions, and more.

It also allows you to download a spreadsheet from Excel that lists all of the videos from your competitors, including upload date, description, title, duration, and day of upload, along with how many views, comments, and likes each video has. Mess around with conditional formatting and filters within the spreadsheet, and you can learn even more about competitor tactics. Make sure that you look into more than one channel before attempting to use these reports for your video creation.

How Can You Get People to Share Your Content?

Each time you put a video up on your channel, you have made an asset toward your content that must be promoted properly across your channels of social media. Making use of the RSS feeds on your channel, you may share your content to many different channels of social media using a channel that is semi-automated. Here is a tool that can help you with that:

DrumUp:

This handy tool allows you to schedule items on your feed with just a simple click, putting them up on your social media. This tool allows you to add more than one Twitter account, more than one Facebook page, and also your LinkedIn profile. You are able to promote your video content in all places in a much more efficient manner. It also allows you to:

- Schedule your videos fast using their one-click schedule button. This distributes them across your different social media platforms.

- Preview what your snippets will appear like on social media once they have been posted to the platforms.

- Authenticate your various accounts on social media.

As you can see, there are plenty of tools to make use on for improving your YouTube channel, stats, and views.

Don't be afraid to do some extra research outside of this book to find even more sources.

Chapter 2:

How to Increase your YouTube Views and Earnings

If YouTube is just a place you go to listen to music or watch cute cat videos, you are seriously holding yourself back on the advantages it can bring you. This can be used as a powerful tool for business to strengthen your online presence and make your brand better-known.

The Three YouTube Channel Types:

Countless resources exist on the topic of YouTube and the different ways you can use it for maximizing your business (and income), but this section will focus specifically on the advantages of branding your channel.

1. **Custom Branded:** This type of channel allows for a website-like interface. However, this probably won't happen for you unless you have a gigantic budget.

2. **Branded:** This option offers the ability to make an experience for audience members that are more

customized than the user channel, which is the most basic.

3. **User:** This is the simplest type of channel. Your videos come with analytics, and you can only customize background images and colors.

Benefits to Setting up a Brand for your YouTube Channel:

Setting up a brand for your YouTube channel shouldn't be done just because. However, you can do this (and should) if you have clear objectives, goals, and a strategy to implement. You also need to already have some videos, so if you aren't to that stage yet, come back to this section once you are. If you do this right, you can enjoy the following benefits:

- **Consistency for your Customers:** When your channel on YouTube is branded, your page can be customized, making your page more consistent in terms of how it compares to your website. You will be able to add background pictures and banners, along with additional tabs and customized sections for content. In addition, a YouTube channel that is branded will give you more optimization opportunities, helping your business get more visibility.

  Remember that YouTube is number two in terms of the world's biggest search engines. YouTube's tagging option lets you add keywords to every video, communicating the subject of your content to search engines. In addition, YouTube comes with its own version of Analytics for you to monitor the performance of other successful videos, visits, and more.

- **Expands your Outreach Socially:** One of the best benefits of YouTube for marketing is how well it integrates with other platforms, including Tumblr, Pinterest, and Twitter. You can add links to those channels on your brand banner, letting audience members find your other content.

Need More Views on YouTube?

YouTube is a great method for getting your expertise and message out to a wider audience. But no body is going to find out about your expertise and message if no one looks at your videos. As the views accumulate, more and more people will learn about you, and you will then get more sales, subscribers, and followers across other platforms. As mentioned, you need to be consistent with your video publishing schedule. When people know to expect a video from you each week or month, they will come back to your channel to see it. Here are some other tips for getting more YouTube views:

Have Plenty of Content: Your very first YouTube video might be quality enough for a single subscriber, but your audience isn't going to just watch the same video every time they go online You must make new videos on a frequent basis, so your viewers and subscribers have content to choose from.

- **Hint at other Videos in your Content:** You should feature other video content of yours within the

last seconds of your videos. After YouTube viewers watch videos, some may lose their attention span in the process of searching for something else to watch. When videos end, more options come up. As soon as an audience member sees these other options, they might go to that, leaving your channel.

Plan for this by including some links to similar videos on your channel at the end of each video you make. This allows your viewers to find more of your content. When other options are simpler to access, you will get more views.

- **Let Viewers Know you:** When audience members find your videos and see them initially, they aren't going to know anything about your videos, channel, or brand. You can fix this by telling them your name, what you do, and more about your business or project at the start of every video.

- **Utilize YouTube Comments:** When you comment on people's YouTube content, people will see your profile name and create YouTube channel backlinks. These links will lead to a higher number of views for you, eventually.

- **Make a FAQ Video:** Every successful YouTube video creator should have a FAQ video that allows you to answer frequently asked questions your audience might have. Ultimately, your audience members are the ones who choose to link to your content on their Twitter, or who they will share your videos with on Facebook. When you make a video that involves frequently asked questions and their answers, it increases the likelihood that people will share it.

Making the Most of Video Descriptions:

Returning to the SEO involved in content on YouTube, the descriptions in your videos shouldn't ever be neglected. This section will allow you to be more easily found online and will also let people know what you create videos about. However, you don't have to overdo this part. A super detailed video description doesn't make a lot of sense since it won't all show when someone loads your video. Just as we mentioned with your video titles, make sure you include keywords for the video in the video description, but keep it simple, authentic, and natural.

Using Meta Tags:

You can utilize Google Keyword Planner to get some ideas on which keywords you should include in your content. These keywords can then be added to the videos you make which will allow you to be more easily found on YouTube and Google. Keep in mind that trying to use too many keywords will have a negative impact on your views, but that a few well-placed and researched keywords can aid you in your ratings and rankings on YouTube. A low number of videos doesn't always mean the content is poor, but it does mean that discovering it is harder and less likely.

Metadata plays a large role in helping your content show up when people search. Look up some videos that are well-converting to see which tags they are putting on their videos. This should give you a few ideas but make sure you don't copy them as this will not help you at all. Remember to be unique and creative!

End in a Positive and Memorable Fashion:

No matter what type of videos you make, they should always be ended in a positive and memorable way.

- **What to Include in the End:** Just as you should always have a standard intro to your videos, you should also make a recognizable outro. Ask the viewers if they liked the video, ask them to subscribe and leave comments and tell them to look at your blog or website.

- **Don't be Afraid to Ask:** No matter which approach you take, keep in mind that those who don't ask never get told yes. Make sure that the ending to your videos is always confident and that you humbly thank your viewers for following you. End smiling and make it so that your audience wants to return to see more of you.

Collaboration with Other YouTube Content Creators:

Lately, a lot of YouTube video creators collaborate with each other, but why is that? Collaboration is beneficial for everyone involved, including the audience, you, and the person you work with.

- **Reaching Out:** Creativity is a constructive process, and when you see other YouTube video creators as competition and nothing else, this will only hold you back. Why not try to reach out to them and work together instead? That way, their success is your success and vice versa. This will help you access a wider audience, and your collaborator will enjoy the same privilege, then your viewers can all get some extra value.

- **Keeping it Fresh:** Working with other YouTube video creators is also a way that you can keep your content fresh and interesting. Surprise your viewers by offering them something completely new!

Always Interact with the Viewers:

Social media is all about interacting and connecting with other people and how much you can show them you care. When your viewers can tell that you actually care about who they are, they will return the favor for you. Listen to what they request, interact with them, and read and respond to comments on your videos. It's true that YouTube has plenty of anger and backlash in the comments sections, but ignore the haters and thank your faithful viewers by giving them the time of day. This will lead to respect and trust.

Chapter 3: How to Increase Viewing Time on Videos

Did you know that people use YouTube for learning about services and products more than other social networks, such as Facebook? What this means is that for those of you who review or sell products, YouTube is a must for your business marketing. Most customers wish to both hear someone explain and see what a product looks like, so they know what to expect. YouTube can provide the answers to these specific questions. If you still are trying to decide how to use YouTube, you can review products through affiliate marketing.

Promoting your Own Items:

Another method for generating income using YouTube is the promotion of your own items or products. A lot of costly training programs have come out online. Certain ones cost $90, and others cost $900. You can run a promotion for your affiliate link for a costly product or training course using your own YouTube videos, and this can earn you big bucks. If you were able to sell a training course for $900 and earn $450 for every sale you make, this would add up a lot over time.

It's true that AdSense can help you make money using YouTube, but that's not the only way to do it. Actually, for a new YouTube video creator, promoting items and products is a faster method for earning a good income, so I recommend starting with this if you're new to the game. True, ads can make some money each day, but affiliate links are better at first. Remember that you shouldn't only stick to one method. Promoting your items, using affiliate links, and AdSense should all be explored.

YouTube Allows Anyone to Begin:

YouTube is great because even amateurs can have their own channel. Out of every method for creating videos online out there, YouTube is by far the simplest.

- **No Learning Curve:** No technical skill is required to do this. You shouldn't have to worry about learning a bunch of technical stuff when you want to make videos with value in them.

  Handheld YouTube Video Creation: YouTube allows you the easy way of sharing valuable content and makes it as easy as just uploading your file and describing it, then hitting publish. This can even be

- done from a handheld device. Use your iPad to upload content and stop worrying about whether you are doing something right. Just focus on creating great videos.

Increasing Viewing Time on YouTube:

A lot of people are still stuck on finding methods for getting more YouTube clicks on their videos, believing that this is what makes content go viral. While this was once true, it no longer is. Now, the length of time a person watches the video counts more. What this means is that if you got a million views, but for each view, people only stayed at your video for seven seconds, then it's not considered engaging enough for YouTube to note or promote your content. Now, how long you can keep someone watching is what counts as viral on the website. How can you keep people watching your videos? Follow the tips below:

- **Aim for More Subscribers:** The people who are subscribed to your channel will be the main people staying for your entire videos.

- **Make your Introduction Professional:** The way your introduction is will control how people react to your videos, as a whole. If your introduction is professional and friendly, people are going to like your content more; it's as simple as that.

- **Shorten Your Content:** How do you think people would rather get their information, by sitting through something for an hour, or for two minutes? We've said this before, but the shorter your videos are, the better.

- **Get More Than One Camera Angle:** Using more than one camera angle helps a lot. If you do this,

messing up is not a problem because you can just keep your video going with the alternate camera. Right when you realize that you were rambling on a bit too much during your video, you can cease the first angle recording and then just switch to recording from the other one. Keep in mind that when people ramble in YouTube videos, people usually don't keep watching them.

- **The Content Must be good:** Keep in mind that your content has to be good and that no amount of special effects or expensive equipment can make up for the lack of valuable content. People won't watch a video that is bad just because the factors above are included. You have to always work on making your videos better and better. Sure, they might be good, but how can they be great?

Prove that People like you: The next step involves showing people that you are liked and popular. Most people think that viewership really affects the way

- YouTube puts videos into rank. What this means is that most believe popularity is counted by views on your videos. If one of your videos has 3,000 views, people are more likely to watch it all the way through since others have already watched them. So even though keeping people on your video matters more than the clicks you get, clicks do matter too.

Lengthening how long people stay on your videos will put you at a higher rank on the search engine of YouTube, where you can access more audience members who could potentially subscribe. In other words, don't skip this part if you want a successful YouTube channel!

Video Challenges and Giveaways:

Everyone likes giveaways. You should offer audience members a reward for being dedicated and engaged with your channel. A video contest or free giveaway is a way to reward the ones that are already following you while drawing in potential subscribers and followers. Giveaways can include some of the following items:

- T-shirts.
- Tech gadgets.
- Hosting subscriptions.

- CDs.

- A free e-book.

These are just a few ideas. Whatever you decide to give away, your viewers will appreciate the opportunity to receive something free and will be likelier to share about your channel to their friends. This is free, viral promotion for your YouTube channel. In order to organize a large giveaway, a lot of hosts on YouTube call for each audience member to follow their profiles on social media in order to be accepted for the drawing. This approach is recommended. It's a good idea if the item you are giving has something to do with your channel topic, but you can do it even if it isn't.

More on Cross Platform Marketing:

Promoting across different platforms is not just recommended, it's a necessity for YouTube marketing. Now that we are well into the social media age being active and present on more than one social profile is a must for existing. If you want your brand to get recognition, you have to be discoverable, meaning activity on social media is required. Make a profile on Google Plus, one on Twitter, and of course, one on Facebook if you aren't already signed up.

In addition, don't forget about the lesser-used platforms such as Snap Chat, Instagram, and Pinterest. If you don't like the idea of having to dedicate a lot of time to this pursuit, try looking into auto-scheduling for your posts which will keep you organized. You can also try out Google Ads and Facebook Ads to further your marketing. In the modern age, this is how you build a successful business and brand. Visibility across the web sets you up with a ubiquitous presence.

Aggressive Marketing:

In order to get more subscribers and make an income with YouTube, you have to be aggressive in your approach to getting successful. The idea that building it up first and that the followers will flow in naturally doesn't always work with social media due to the amount of competition present. You have to actively promote yourself and your channel

as much as you can. A YouTube channel that is growing in popularity will help you stay motivated to keep going, making valuable video content for your viewers.

Tell your friends about what you're doing, asking them to subscribe if they want to. Keep in mind that pestering people will have the opposite effect that you are going for. Get online and make personal connections, then ask them to subscribe and like without being annoying about it.

Chapter 4:

What Matters Most for Getting Subscribers?

When you are building a business, you have to draw in your audience using more than basic sales tactics. Trust matters a lot when you want to draw in customers. If your customers don't respect or trust you, you aren't going to have any luck. Therefore, you have to take the time to build up trust and rapport with the audience and customers. When you do this, you will have an advantage over other businesses and help your list of subscribers grow. When you upload video content to YouTube, you are giving your customers reasons to evaluate and look at your products and services.

Credibility and YouTube Marketing:

Credibility arises when someone has all the information needed. There isn't a more direct, more easily absorbed, or simpler way to show information than using YouTube videos. Just 20 seconds of content is a lot more engaging and offers more value than a whole page of text or marketing content.

- **Showing Satisfied Customers:** The best way to build up your credibility and trust using videos is to put videos up on your channel of people recommending your product and proof of client engagement. For potential customers, a satisfied client giving their opinion is the most convincing piece of evidence that your brand is worthwhile.

- **Winning New Clients:** Proving the way you respect and treat your existing customers is going to help you gain new ones. Videos which show customers enjoying your brand or showing how good it is will engage new viewers and subscribers. Testimonials on your channel will build up trust by demonstrating and displaying the value in a way that is engaging and meaningful in a way that other ads could never be. Small or large, any business needs to use video content to build and establish their business and products.

One simple method for doing this is putting a video up that has instructions or information steps, targeting your audience with success and accomplishing a set of actions or tasks. As newer social networks, such as Blab and Periscope pop up, older websites seem to pale in comparison. YouTube is an example of this, in some cases. Although it's still wildly popular, people might fear that YouTube isn't going to be as popular pretty soon.

The fact is that YouTube has existed for very long, leading people to believe that newer websites make more sense to put their time and effort into. Although the newer sites are valuable and useful in their own way, it isn't smart to exclude YouTube from your current strategy of marketing.

The Three Most Important Factors on YouTube:

If your desire is to create a YouTube channel that is successful and shows your niche, you must already know how to create a successful brand and channel. To be more specific, you have to be aware of the three consideration that is most important on YouTube.

1. Your Quantity of Subscribers:

A lot of interested, quality subscribers and viewers is your ideal YouTube audience. Quality, interested subscribers, means anyone who is already interested in the niche you are involved with. They are already subscribed to other channels that are somewhat related to the niche you're in and like watching a lot of videos about that subject.

Appeal plus Marketing: Attaining a higher number of subscribers means creating a channel that is appealing and combining that with the correct form of marketing. It does help to have an existing audience outside your videos, but you don't need this. It's possible to leverage the audiences of other people's challenges by interviewing experts in your niche, leaving comments on

- related video content, and more. However, when you choose to try to go leverage the audiences of other channels, you can only enjoy success if you choose to have a "win-win" attitude.

- **Commenting on Videos:** You can get more exposure by commenting, while your comments offer more social proof and exposure for the videos. This is a win-win situation for you and the video creator.

- **Interviewing Experts:** Seeking out information from existing experts in the field will help you get more exposure and credibility (especially if the person also does promotion for the interview). This offers a win-win for you and the expert. Other methods exist for getting a higher number of subscribers, but the best approach is to find a couple that work best for you, then focus on those.

2. How Long the Videos are Watched:

YouTube has intentionally emphasized that when they think about videos viewed, they are also considering how many minutes of video are watched. This is partially to help against spam since people can just purchase views. These fake views are dishonest and make video content appear better to possible audience members. But these videos will likely not appear high up in the search results of YouTube. To get a higher rank, you need to make videos that people want to watch all the way through, or at least, most of the way through. You can do this with two different methods:

- **Creating Compelling Content:** The first way to get people to watch your videos all the way through is to create compelling content that makes people want to watch. How is this done? You can check out what your successful competitors are doing and look at what works here. Next, check out the retention rate on your own videos to see what works. Don't check out the retention rate of your videos until you've gotten past 100 views. If your retention rate is based on just eight views, this isn't enough information to form any conclusions.

- **Making One Longer Video:** The other method for increasing the length of time your videos are viewed is to of course create a valuable video. However, how long your video is matters, as well. We have already mentioned that when it comes to YouTube subscribers, having shorter videos is better, but this is an exception. Retention rate determines how long someone sits through your video, but how many minutes they watch for matters more. If you want one specific video to get great ratings, you can make it a bit longer.

You can do plenty of planning to prepare for your video if you want to make one specific piece of content longer. For instance, you could do an instructional video on how to develop an exercise routine and make it 25 minutes long instead of four. Using advertising's help, you can get people to watch this video for thousands of minutes. Your average watch time for your videos will go up due to having a longer video that people watch for longer.

It won't matter whether the longer video and another shorter video get the same amount of clicks, but it will matter that people spend more time watching the longer one than the shorter one. Make sure you make compelling content, but for some of them, make longer videos to add to your overall minutes-watched score.

3. How Consistently you Upload Videos:

If you are more consistent with uploading videos, you will also be likelier to gain attention from those subscribed to your channel. A lot of people subscribe to a channel and then forget about it unless you make sure you are consistent with putting out content. The thing about publishing and uploading videos is some audience members will have email notifications turned on, so that each time you put something up, a group of viewers will know. Your subscribers are likelier to remember you if your videos come out on a regular basis. If your videos are uploaded once a week, on Friday afternoons, your audience will be more likely to remember that you and your channel exist.

Some of your subscribers are going to look at your channel regularly to find what you have released most recently. These audience members will usually engage with, watch, and even comment on your video. When they do this, your video will go up in the rankings on YouTube, bringing more traffic through the search engine, too.

The audience members are the ones who will get this momentum flowing for you. But for them to be able to do this, they have to be able to remember your channel, meaning consistency of uploading is key for you.

The Powerful Video Platform:

In our modern world which is increasingly full of social networks, YouTube remains a very powerful platform for your videos. Since we have covered the factors that matter most for building up your subscribers, you can build your channel and videos using this information. Obviously, the most important factor of all is that you create valuable content, but you also need to know how to do this as it relates to SEO on YouTube. Experimenting with plenty of ideas will allow you to find out what works best.

Chapter 5:

How to Win and Keep Subscribers on YouTube

Videos are leading the scene of content marketing as of this year. YouTube is in the lead as far as video blogging goes, along with video marketing and video sharing. The platform is free and offered by the giant search engine, Google. People absolutely love YouTube and use it all the time. Twitter and Facebook have also tried to join the game of video marketing recently but as of yet, have only a tiny fraction of the impact of YouTube. If you already have a channel on YouTube, you might be curious about how to draw more subscribers to your brand as well as increasing how far your videos reach.

Since YouTube has at least a billion visitors each month, a gigantic potential exists for building up your audience, each time you make a new video. This can be a fashion design review video or a skateboard trick tutorial. Either way, YouTube is where people go to find the videos they want. Plenty of brand new YouTube stars are being made every day, so for those seeking publicity and online marketing expansion, it's a must. YouTube is the best way to expand your reach across the online world as a blogger, increasing your connections with readers.

More Tips for Getting Subscribers:

The chances for bloggers to make use of YouTube and bring more traffic to their site is high. In order for this to occur, however, you first need to know how to bring more subscribers to your channel. This detailed section will show you just how to do that. If your main business goal right now is to build up your channel, these tips will help you see tremendous growth within a matter of months.

Make a Script and Plan:

The initial step to making your journey on YouTube successful is to have a plan for your channel and video content. The next step is then to structure how your videos will go. Choose what you like to create and work on getting the skills related to that. Although we mentioned drawing inspiration from your competitor's channels, don't copy what they do. Sticking to what you are passionate about is key for enjoying success with this platform.

> **Writing a Script:** Your video creation will go much smoother if you actually write out a script since this will keep you on track as you speak and make organization much easier. When you make a script to stick with, you will stay on task instead of getting lost in rambles. This will keep your events flowing perfectly and make your

video focused. When you write your script, include the main points to cover, calls to action for your audience (such as subscribing or liking the video), how many words you'll say, and what actions you'll perform while on camera.

- **Identify the Target:** You need to also identify the target audience, structuring your script on their current understanding and level of information. If you're doing tech videos, are you speaking to tech beginners? Are you talking about Americans or non-native speakers of English? Are they intermediate or experts in the field you're discussing? Are you trying to be informative or funny to suit their tastes? Using the right language for your target audience is a must!

Making Entertaining Videos:

We've already discussed the importance of making videos that are valuable to your audience. This is an obvious one, but your content has to be informative, engaging and also entertaining for viewers. And this has to be the case throughout the whole video, not just the intro or ending. If you lose your hook right in the middle of your video, you're going to lose viewers.

Informative Video Content: Content that is most valuable to viewers is both informative and entertaining instead of being just one or the other. With all types of marketing, this is the standard, but with videos, it's especially important. Think about it, if someone wanted to find something out just for its informative properties, why wouldn't they just read an article or get a book on the subject? They are watching videos to receive information in a new, more engaging way.

- **Evergreen and Burst:** More specifically, try to upload a mix of evergreen and burst videos. The burst videos are popular for a short time to get you hits in the short term, but won't stay popular past a certain amount of time. Evergreen content, however, will stay relevant for a long time and get you valuable archived YouTube views. If you can, attempt to make content that is mostly evergreen. If you have a hard time being comfortable in front of a camera, do screen casts, which involve giving information with other images shown.

However, whichever type of videos you focus on, always ensure they are both valuable and highly engaging before you publish them.

Aim for making More Videos:

This might be simpler to say than to do, but it's very valid for the future success of your channel. One of the main reasons people subscribe to YouTube channels is because they appreciate what they see and are expecting more of it.

- **Don't be Forgotten:** Subscribers on YouTube won't usually appreciate channels that are dead or don't make a lot of videos. In our modern age, especially, consumers are always looking for more entertainment, and you must be ready to follow these demands to stay relevant. As we've already mentioned many times in the book, consistency is the only way to create a valuable, lasting relationship to your audience.

- **Stick to Your Schedule:** Try to release your videos according to a strict schedule. One each week is ideal, but you should go for a minimum of one each month. Stay with that schedule and try not to upload anything between, which could hinder your YouTube reputation. People enjoy watching TV series because they can look forward to episodes on certain days. Following this structure will help you be more appealing to viewers.

Be Ruthless in your Editing:

With your YouTube videos, you need to be ruthless with your editing. The famous photographer, Thomas Hawk, says that for each picture he publishes, 10 have been rejected. This should apply to all areas of editing, videos included.

Don't Rush the Process: Be ruthless with your editing to make sure that what you publish is only your

- absolute best. If you rush through this for the sake of sticking to your publishing schedule, it's going to hurt your business over time. Instead, adequately prepare and give yourself plenty of wiggle room as far as time goes, so you can select the best content.

- **Ask a Friend:** If you can't tell which shots of you are best for your final video, ask a friend to watch with you and help you decide which ones are upload-ready.

- **Do Plenty of Recordings:** Whenever you decide to shoot a video, do plenty of recordings and only select the best ones. Take a lot of shots until you find one that you are confident about. You can edit with Adobe Premier for Windows. The right editing tools will help a lot with this and depending on how serious you want to get about it, you could hire someone to help you edit.

Always Explore and Experiment:

This is meant to be a fun experiment, so don't forget to keep exploring to find what works best for you, personally! Someone else's methods may not work the best for you, so find your own. Experiment with backgrounds, camera angles, thumbnails, and the rest of the methods given to you throughout this book, then track the changes you make and how they impact your audience's reactions. Stick with your business and brand, always staying true to it. Keep in mind that creating something valuable using YouTube requires perseverance, time, and effort. But if you're committed, you'll see the benefits in no time.

Chapter 6:

Creating Winning, Profitable YouTube Content

If you're one of the millions of users on YouTube every day, watching videos, it's about time you started creating your own content. Instead of being a passenger, you can be a pilot. YouTube allows people to create their own videos, upload them, and become discovered on a larger scale than was ever possible before. In fact, many celebrities have been discovered this way. The revenue and viewership are small at first, but if you stick to your plan and promote your channel, it could become one of the popular ones on YouTube, bringing you a great income.

Getting people's attention is not the same as keeping it, which is why YouTube has changed its system of ranking videos. The videos that hold the attention of viewers the longest are going to get higher rankings than the ones who get people to click on them. This should help you feel more motivated to create quality videos. So how can you improve this to make your channel more successful? Follow these tips for creating a stronger engagement with your viewers, improving your ranking.

Don't Game the System:

There's no point in trying to gain a higher ranking by bypassing YouTube's algorithms. As soon as someone believes they have beaten this, it could change. Instead, focus your efforts on researching keywords, crafting the right titles, and making videos consistently, as mentioned before. Producing valuable content consistently will give you the results you want.

Know Who's Watching:

Knowing your audience is the next key to success on YouTube. You should know how old the people watching are, what they enjoy doing, which words will get them to pay attention, what they want to learn, and which benefits they're hunting for. This is simple stuff, but it is often overlooked by people. You should never assume that you already know the needs of your audience without doing proper research to find out. Here is how to maximize your relationship with your viewers on YouTube:

- **Offer Incentives for Staying:** Your viewers should know within under 30 seconds why they must stay on your channel. Let them know what you can offer them and then prove it throughout the rest of your video.

  Pre-production Planning: Great videos don't just occur by chance. They need pre-production planning. This includes a shot list, a list of props for each scene, a story board, and any additional

- footage needed to bring your video to life in the editing stages.

- **Be Energetic:** Those who are enthusiastic on their videos are far likelier to keep the attention of their viewers than someone who is dull and monotonous. You can study this by watching stand-up comics, watching how their energy has an impact on viewers. Try to talk louder than you usually would and gesture a little more exaggeratedly. This might feel a little awkward at first but usually, results in a more exciting end product that will draw viewers in more.

Don't be Afraid to Take Risks:

As soon as you know who your audience members are, go with your intuition and don't be afraid to take calculated risks. Every niche has a bunch of untested assumptions, so test out common beliefs. This will show viewers that you aren't afraid to think outside of the box and you may learn a few things along the way. In addition, make sure you are paying attention to descriptions and headlines in your videos. Your content might be great, but if it doesn't have the correct keywords in the tags and headlines, people won't find it! Use the keyword tool on Google to find out whether the words you selected are popular or not. Try to find a minimum of 10k searches globally that are "low competition."

Chapter 7:

YouTube Marketing, the Next Step

The far reach and convenience offered by the Internet has offered countless people the chance to earn their living digitally. This involves the chance to monetize nearly every opportunity, talent, or skill. And as with any other venture for making money, plenty of misinformation is out there on the topic, including YouTube marketing. More specifically, the name YouTube comes up a lot in articles that talk about earning income from home. But although you can make income using this platform, it usually doesn't happen in the way people believe it will. Actually, to be successful with this, you must establish a strategy that is more sustainable, which requires digging below the surface.

Earning Income with YouTube- the Challenges:

The myth of YouTube says that all you have to do to earn money is put up some videos, bring viewers to your channel, and then make money from the advertisements on the videos. Does this sound effortless or too good to be true? That's because it's both. This is the story that everyone repeats, but the truth is that ad revenue won't bring you the income you seek. Even for advertisers that do pay a lot for the promotion of their services using ads, only a tiny amount of this goes to the creators.

To put it another way, for each million views, you won't make more than a thousand dollars or so. And getting to this many views is a lot harder than it sounds! Thankfully, ads on YouTube are far from the only way to generate income for yourself, as long as you are willing to come up with a plan and work hard.

Other Options for Making an Income on YouTube:

To get started with making good money on YouTube, you shouldn't view it as a medium that is monetize-able on its own and should instead view it as a useful catalyst. The best way to earn an income using YouTube is to use its gigantic network of users. Follow these tips to do that:

- **Using Shopify:** As we've mentioned a few times, YouTube is the world's second biggest search engine, after Google. Considering this from the viewpoint of marketing, it just doesn't make a lot of sense to not take advantage of that. One great opportunity for making money is using YouTube as a platform for selling your own merchandise. Perhaps you already have some merchandise to try to sell. You can use Shopify to set up your storefront online, then make videos related to the niche your product is in. Once the videos are over, include a link to your shop's landing page.

This process involves more than just that, but a good product can be sold much easier with simple videos. You can product how-to videos or simple question and answer style content.

Using Yondo: If you have a goal to earn money from your YouTube videos, you can take advantage of a much better choice than relying on ad revenue. Start with making a channel on YouTube and gaining subscribers. The goal here is to build your brand up while engaging with your viewers. As soon as your reputation is solid, you can start directing traffic to your blog or selling page where you can sell premium video content. You can use solutions such as Yondo to do this, which will allow you to make a store that sells video content.

Your free content on YouTube will pull people in and those who want to see more will have the chance to buy more. Your videos can sell as rentals on a pay per view purpose, subscriptions by the month, and more. You will set your own price and don't have to split the profits with YouTube.

Affiliate Linking: Affiliate marketing is a highly popular method of making money online. The problem with that is that a lot of marketers doing this aren't going about it the right way. Rather than using your blog to get traffic to your affiliate links, create a channel on YouTube instead. This is much more engaging and

- entertaining for people. The internet appears to be moving toward a preference for videos over text, meaning that you won't get left in the dust.

- **Using YouTube for Sponsorships:** The YouTube video creators who have enjoyed the most success

include advertisements and sponsorships in their videos. The makers of these videos have found these opportunities on their own, more often than not. The best thing about this is that YouTube won't take a cut of your earnings. In addition, you can make your own contracts based on your goals and audience size instead of working under YouTube's terms.

Usually, how much revenue is generated through this method depends on how hard you work and almost always ends up being more than ad revenue from YouTube alone. Keep in mind that you can still work on getting ad revenue in the meantime, drawing on two different sources of money from just one video.

Consider Live Speaking: You can leverage your reputation on YouTube by transitioning into live speaking. If your channel is involved with a specific audience or niche, conduct some research regarding related industry events or annual conferences that need speakers. You can then pull together your best clips and YouTube statistics, creating a pitch and package to show

- to event directors. Speaking engagements, such as these, can earn you a lot of money, even with just an hour-long talk. Ensure that you aren't missing out on this opportunity, which can then grow your audience even more.

The tips above help you to use YouTube as a tool, not as the "end all be all." YouTube can be one stepping stone on the way to success for you and a catalyst to make your dreams come true.

Think Creatively:

As with any other venture, you should never be afraid to think creatively. The guidelines in this book are just that; guidelines. They aren't rules that you must adhere to if they aren't working for you. Will you be successful with earning money on YouTube? That's up to you.

Conclusion

YouTube is becoming one of the most powerful communication platforms and is far more engaging than other ads. People like to watch videos. It's easy and often entertaining for the audience members. Videos allow you to connect more personally with your followers, offering a hands-on approach to marketing and your brand.

For your marketing to be successful, engagement cannot be skipped out on. Websites that allow you to show videos give you so many opportunities for engagement. The viewers can lead comments on the videos, interacting both with you and each other. They can see your face and hear your voice, making you more trustworthy to them.

Don't forget to craft a memorable intro and outro for your videos. This not only helps you with your brand but helps your video seem more appealing and entertaining to your audience members. This will serve your business and brand, offering the video some professionalism, just like a TV show's main theme song. In addition, an appealing video intro keeps your viewers wanting more. Your outro is your chance to encourage viewers to subscribe!

YouTube humanizes companies, making them more helpful, professional, and approachable. Adding this to your business strategy will help you no matter which industry you're in. If you're ready to take advantage of this, follow the guidelines given to you in this book and if you stick with it, you'll enjoy success with YouTube Marketing.

Finally, if you enjoyed this useful guide, please take the time to leave it a positive review on Amazon. Thank you again and good luck on your YouTube marketing journey!

CPSIA information can be obtained
at www.ICGtesting.com
Printed in the USA
LVHW012320230621
690964LV00016B/1127

9 781914 418051